The Poet's Perspective

Also by Gladys Mary Coles

POETRY

The Sounding Circle
Sinerva and Other Poems
The Snow Bird Sequence
Stoat, in Winter
Liverpool Folio
Studies in Stone
Leafburners: New and Selected Poems
The Glass Island
The Echoing Green
Song of the Butcher Bird

BIOGRAPHY AND CRITICISM

At Beauty Aghast: Gerard Manley Hopkins and his True Arcadia
The Flower of Light: A Biography of Mary Webb
Introductions to Mary Webb's novels *Gone to Earth and Precious Bane*
Introduction to Mary Webb's essays *The Spring of Joy*
Mary Webb: a new biography
Walks with Writers (with Gordon Dickins)
Mary Webb and Her Shropshire World

AS EDITOR

Both Sides of the River: Merseyside in Poetry and Prose
Poet's England: Lancashire
Poet's England: Cheshire
Mary Webb: Collected Prose and Poems
Selected Poems of Mary Webb
The Poet's View: Poems for Paintings in the Walker Art Gallery, Liverpool
Chester: A Collection of Stories (Chester Literature Festival)
Poet's England: Wirral
Making Worlds: 100 Contemporary Women Poets
Poetry Pool: Poems from Liverpool John Moores University
The Mary Webb Society Journal
Between Fields & Stars, New & Selected Poetry & Prose by Edmund Cusick

VIDEO

Secret Shropshire

The Poet's Perspective

Poems for Paintings
in the Walker Art Gallery
Liverpool

Compiled & Edited
by
Gladys Mary Coles

HEADLAND

First published in 2010
by
HEADLAND PUBLICATIONS
38 York Avenue, West Kirby,
Wirral, Merseyside. CH48 3JF

A full CIP record for this book is available
from the British Library

ISBN 978 1 902096 55 1

Printed in Great Britain by
Oriel Studios
Hawthorne Road, Liverpool L20 6NS

HEADLAND acknowledges the financial
assistance of Arts Council England.

ARTS COUNCIL ENGLAND

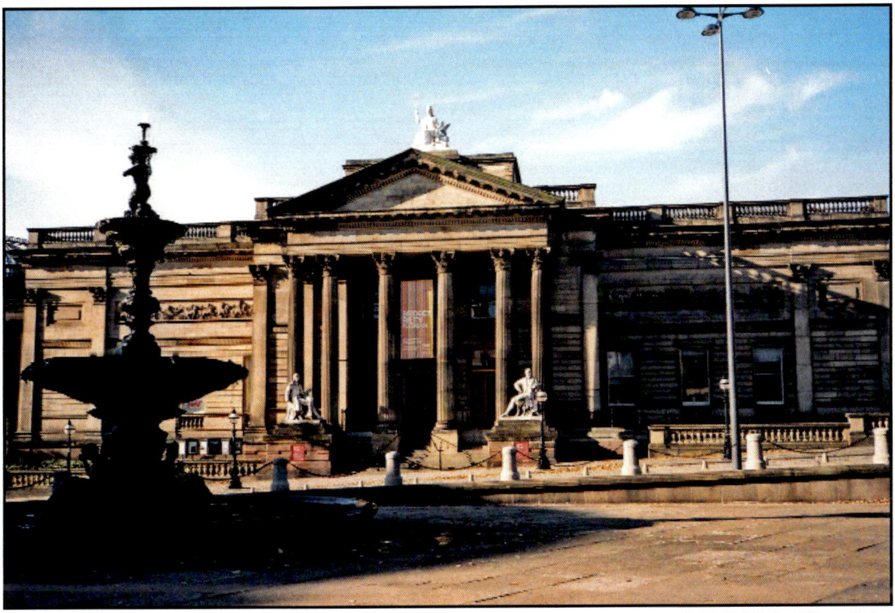

The Walker Art Gallery, Liverpool

The Walker Art Gallery, designed by Cornelius Sherlock, is one of a group of fine Neo-classical buildings in the centre of Liverpool. The gift of Sir Andrew Barclay Walker, an alderman and brewer, it was opened in 1877 by the Earl of Derby to great public rejoicing. The Walker's collections of fine and decorative art soon became the most important in the country, outside London. Some of the earliest purchases, such as 'And when did you last see your Father?' by W. F. Yeames, works by the Pre-Raphaelites, and 'A Street in Brittany' by Stanhope Forbes, are now world famous paintings. The history and growth of the Walker reflect Liverpool's strong cultural tradition and appreciation of the arts.

Adorning the entrance, the statues in Carrara marble of Michelangelo and Raphael, and (on the roof) the symbolic 'Spirit of Liverpool', are by John Warrington Wood. A replica 'Spirit of Liverpool', carved from a 41 ton block of Chinese marble in 1993-4, took the place of the original statue, now housed in the nearby National Conservation Centre.

Today the Walker is part of National Museums Liverpool. For the scope and high quality of its permanent collections and annual series of important temporary exhibitions, it is accepted as the national gallery of the North. In 2008, Liverpool's year as European Capital of Culture, the Walker attracted more than 400,000 visitors.

Gladys Mary Coles

Introduction

In linking the arts of poetry and painting, this anthology belongs in a tradition reaching back to classical antiquity, to critics and philosophers who saw the two as 'Sister Arts'. Aristotle, in his *Poetics*, draws analogies between them – both arts being mimetic of life, a sisterhood of imagery – while he also defines their differences in method. These correspondences and differences, parallel concerns and processes such as close observation, selection of detail and image, and not least composition, 'the common denominator' (as Wallace Stevens said), have been discussed in every age up to the present time.

The relationship between poetry and painting is, for me, of compelling interest, one which I relish exploring, primarily as a poet and, to a lesser degree, as a visual artist. In developing my twin passions, the Walker Art Gallery has been an enormously formative influence from my schooldays onwards, a kind of *alma mater* and, with its rich collections of art of every period from the Middle Ages through to the contemporary world, a 'heaven-haven' (to use an image from Gerard Manley Hopkins).

The present volume follows my earlier anthology of poems written in response to paintings in the Walker – *The Poet's View* (Headland 1996), a popular book including work by Seamus Heaney, Wendy Cope and Dannie Abse. This was the result of workshops I held at the Gallery, for both a poetry writing course I was tutoring at Liverpool University and a summer series for the public. Since then I have led numerous workshops at the Walker, some on occasions such as National Poetry Day, others with my students from Liverpool John Moores University (six of these, now graduates, have poems in this book).

Deciding to compile and edit a second anthology, I began by making a selection of the paintings I wished to include, then embarked on the process of matching poets to paintings. Some of the poems arose from my workshops attended by local poets, and others were written in direct response to invitations I sent to internationally known poets such as Roger McGough, Brian Patten, Ian McMillan, Anne Stevenson, U.A. Fanthorpe and others. The poem which U.A. Fanthorpe wrote to Holman Hunt's 'The Eve of St Agnes' was, sadly, to be one of her last. I have also included two pieces of 'flash fiction' (a short form close to poetry), and a 'Mini Period Drama'.

Facing each poem is the painting or sculpture which inspired it. I arranged the anthology chronologically, following the date of composition of the work of art, and aimed to represent all the periods and schools of painting in the Walker's collections. I selected four winners of the John Moore s Contemporary Painting Prize (from the John Moores Exhibitions founded in 1957 and today a major strand in the Liverpool Biennial).

Of the forty-eight works of art reproduced here, one is an intricate French ivory carving of the mid-fourteenth century (a small 'home altarpiece'), and two are sculptures – a bust by Epstein, and Gibson's magnificent 'The Tinted Venus' (centrepiece of the Walker's Sculpture Gallery).

A painting offers the viewer an intimacy, something actual and contained, but more than a visual experience, something transcending form and colour, texture, light and shadow. In their verbal responses and interpretations, poets need to engage with that intimacy and 'truly inhabit' the painting (in Dannie and Joan Abse's phrase), yet retain their own artistic and imaginative freedom.

In this anthology, the poems and adjacent reproductions of paintings and sculpture will provide arresting juxtapositions, one illuminating the other and bringing new perspectives to the reader, extended enjoyment.

Gladys Mary Coles

I am grateful for assistance of various kinds to staff at the Walker and National Museums Liverpool. In particular I wish to thank Reyahn King, Director of Art Galleries, for her interest in this project. My thanks also to Nicky Fawcett, Public Programmes Officer, for help in arranging my workshops on Poetry and Creative Writing at the Walker during recent years. I am indebted to Stephen White, Assistant Curator of Fine Art, and to Nathan Pendlebury, Administration Officer, for his assistance in securing the photographic images. I would also like to thank Kate Johnson, Andrew Dickey, and Helen Young.

My gratitude also to Dr Julian Treuherz, Frank Milner and Peter Betts; and to Catherine Marcangeli and Adrian Mealing.

For their interest in my work, I extend thanks to Dr Tamsin Spargo, Director of the School of Media, Critical and Creative Arts at Liverpool John Moores University, and to Alison Hughes and Joan Squires at Liverpool University's Department of Continuing Education and Professional Development.

In my search for copyright owners I received help from Martha Lineman at the Bridgeman Art Library, Christine Cauldwell at DACS, staff at Tate Images, Beverley Art Gallery, York Art Gallery, Victoria Miro Gallery, and the Lowry Gallery. And special thanks to John Kavanagh for his wonderful artwork on this book.

To all the poets whose work is included here I express my enduring gratitude.

ACKNOWLEDGEMENTS

Every effort has been made to trace and contact the owners of copyright material in this book. In the event of any question arising as to the use of any material, the publisher, while expressing regret for any errors or omissions, will be pleased to take the necessary steps to amend these and to make corrections in any future editions of the book.

Grateful acknowledgement is made for permission given by the copyright owners, agencies and managers of Estates of artists, for the reproduction of images of the following works:

'A Street in Brittany' and 'Off to the Fishing Grounds' by Stanhope Alexander Forbes © Bridgeman Art Library. Courtesy of National Museums Liverpool, Walker Art Gallery.

'Madame Hessel on the Sofa' by Edouard Vuillard © ADAGP, Paris and DACS, London 2009. Courtesy of National Museums Liverpool, Walker Art Gallery.

'Portrait of Pau Cucurny with a Dog, 1903' by Pablo Picasso © Succession Picasso / DACS 2009. Courtesy of National Museums Liverpool, Walker Art Gallery.

'Fancy Dress, Miss Beerbohm, 1916' by Walter Sickert © Estate of Walter Sickert. All rights reserved, DACS 2009. Courtesy of National Museums Liverpool, Walker Art Gallery.

'Israfel' by Sir Jacob Epstein © Estate of Sir Jacob Epstein. Courtesy of Tate Images. Courtesy of National Museums Liverpool, Walker Art Gallery.

'The Fever Van' by L.S. Lowry © Estate of L.S. Lowry 2009. © Courtesy National Museums Liverpool, Walker Art Gallery.

'Springtime in Eskdale' by James McIntosh Patrick © Bridgeman Art Library. Courtesy of National Museums Liverpool, Walker Art Gallery.

'Baby in pram in garden' and 'Three Self-portraits with a White Wall' by John Bratby © Bridgeman Art Library. Courtesy of National Museums Liverpool, Walker Art Gallery.

'Meat Painting II - In Memoriam Renee Magritte' by Adrian Henri © Estate of Adrian Henri. Courtesy of National Museums Liverpool, Walker Art Gallery.

For kind permission to reproduce images of paintings in which the copyright is held by the artist:

'Cow Mutations' © Tim Head. Courtesy of National Museums Liverpool, Walker Art Gallery.

'Blotter' © Peter Doig. Courtesy of National Museums Liverpool, Walker Art Gallery.

'Before Vermeer's Clouds' © Martin Greenland. Courtesy of National Museums Liverpool, Walker Art Gallery.

Photographic images © National Museums Liverpool, Walker Art Gallery.

Winners of the John Moores Contemporary Painting Prize:
John Bratby, *Three Self-portraits with a White Wall*, 1957.
Tim Head, *Cow Mutations*, 1987.
Peter Doig, *Blotter*, 1993.
Martin Greenland, *Before Vermeer's Clouds*, 2006.

'After Edgehill, 1642' by Gladys Mary Coles, a major prize winner in the Cardiff International Poetry Competition, was first published in the *Faber Book of English History in Verse,* and reprinted in her collection *Song of the Butcher Bird* (Flambard 2007).

Contents

To Lindsay, Kathryn
and Howard

Ut pictura poesis

~ Horace

(*Ars Poetica*)

Christ Discovered in the Temple, 1342, Simone Martini (c.1284-1344)

CHRIST DISCOVERED IN THE TEMPLE

A sword shall pierce your soul...
that the thoughts of many hearts may be revealed
- Luke 2:35, 41-52

Mary holds, inscribed in Latin,
words which express her woe,
her fear
for her divinely mortal son.

Before his understanding fully formed,
before his wisdom flowed with grace
like water becoming wine,

the child remained in the temple
surrounded by scholars, doctors –
none as wise as He
yet so many years more learned.

Mary and Joseph sought him, anxious,
but the child was about his Father's business.

Here he stands –
jewel spun silk
and naked feet,
the feet to walk
on water and over
the palmed path to Golgotha
and forty days further.

This is the third
of Seven Sorrows,
the fifth joyful mystery
of Our Lady's rosary.

Hannah Todd

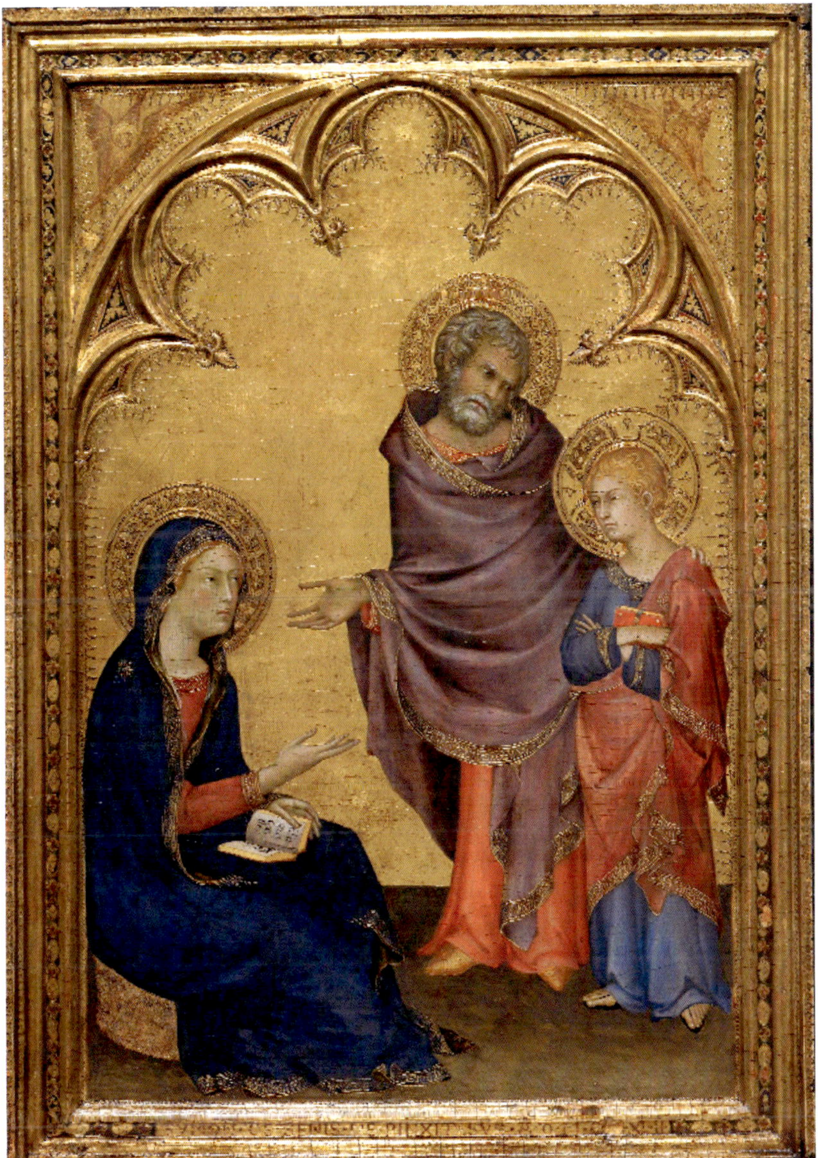

French Ivory Home Altarpiece, c. 1350

IVORY DIPTYCH

Write the Lord's prayer on a dime; tiny forms
stand in for large and eternal matters, ancient
ivory, a few inches, a palm's width of creamy stone,
of animal flesh and bone, a pale tile, glossed, cryptic.

The tiny figures' tableaux of the Virgin's life
freeze her moments of conception, birth, adoration;
gold and spice poured on her child, the amazing
boy who stands on her lap, blessing with fingers,
no bigger than rose spines. Then bereavement

and sorrow, supported by friends; at last
crowned with glory among rollicking clouds.
Angels surround her, peep from crevices,
Gothic arcades, rolls of cloth; tiny hands busy
with harps and pipes, handing out scrolls, pointing.

This teeming market place for souls hard-sells
devotion, road signs to ever rarer heights.
We close the limbed tablets, and beams turn off
in our hands. Put away this Ipod for contemplation,
in further lone, wise moments, inner researches.

Susan Craggs

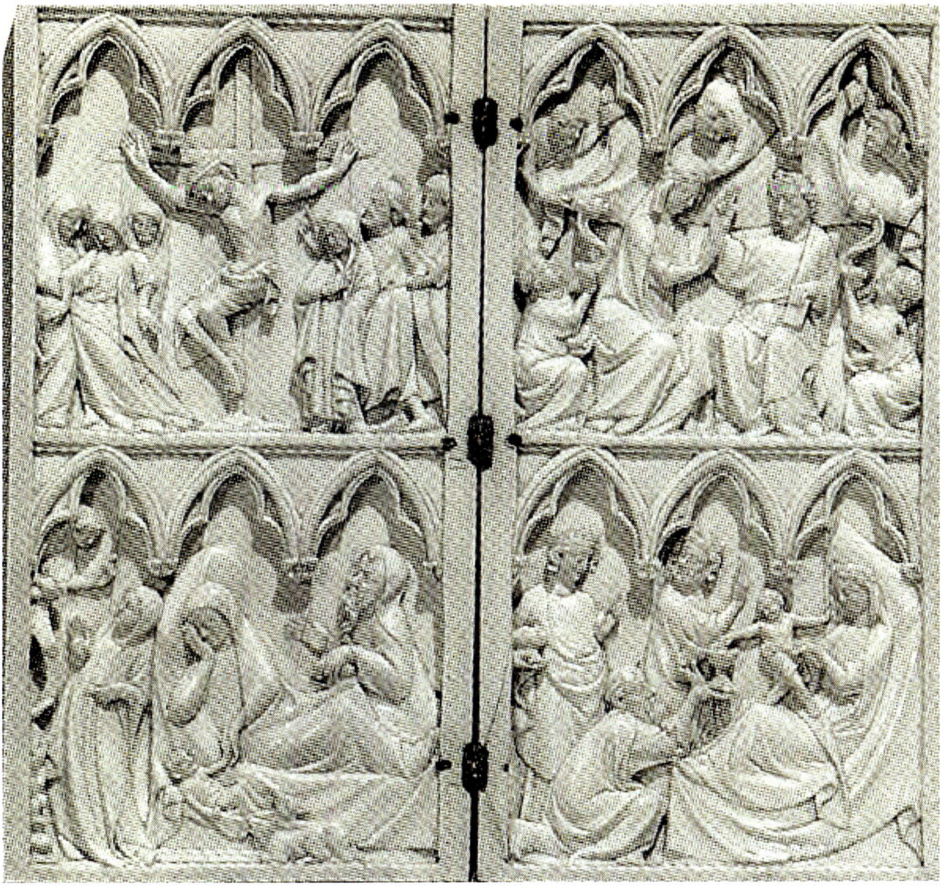

Birth of the Virgin, c.1470, Pietro Vannucci, called Perugino (1450-1523)

MATERIAL

Her mouth is dry from calling
a name on the night's ripped distance;
stars shattered against
ongoing dawn –
for now is silence
but for the child's
hoping, the paint cracked
and dry,
flakes meshed to the idea
of presence
three slow breaths
or soft steps in the hour after sunrise;
and what was before is almost absent
lost in shadow,
in the midwives' procession
in from outside;
him in the country's hills
asleep on a haystack or
digging the vineyards,
propagating a son,
or him in the servants' kitchen
skinning bones for the feast to come.
He is striding through their sentences,
syntax, cerebral cortex,
as the sun ticks over a whole day's work
observed with eyes wet in a summer rain,
the horizon line a journey
away from themselves
and into time.

Eleanor Rees

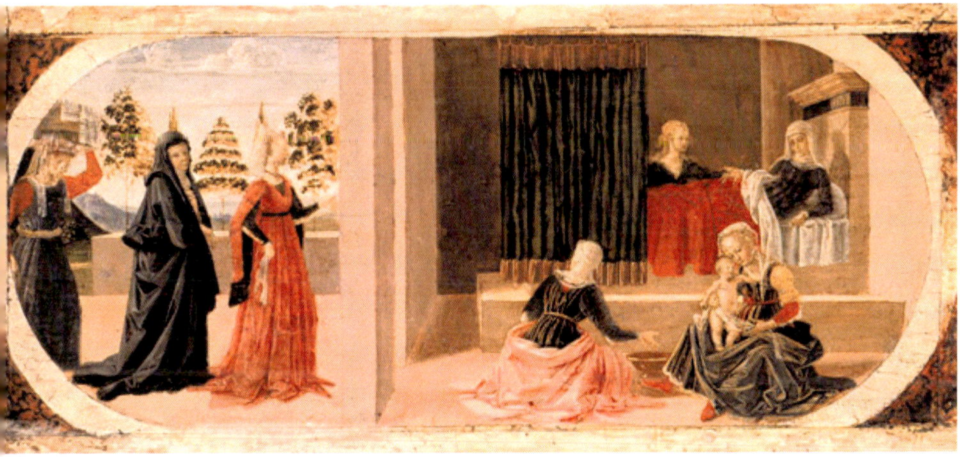

Supper at Emmaus, c.1533, Titian (c.1485-1576)

Luke, 24: 13-32

THE REVENANT

And if you did come back, I would know you
in whatever stage of your lifetime's flesh and shape.
Or if you appeared, a visible ghost, here
yet not here, even then I would know you.
Or if you returned in another's human form –
as Jesus did on that third day, appearing
to his disciples on the dusty road to Emmaus
but unrecognized, a stranger to their eyes –
if you came back in any form, surely
I would know you, sense your caring presence.

And if, just once more, I could serve you supper,
there'd be your favourite bread, cool butter,
chicken and wine, some green-grey beans,
and I'd scatter blue borage flowers across the table
to stave off sadness. Yet I would know,
the day nearly over, I'd have to face that moment
when you'd vanish from my sight –
as Jesus did, at supper in Emmaus, seconds after
his disciples recognized him in the pilgrim-stranger
as he blessed the bread and broke it.

I'd want to freeze that instant before you'd fade,
catch your words on the evening air –
I will be with you, always.

Gladys Mary Coles

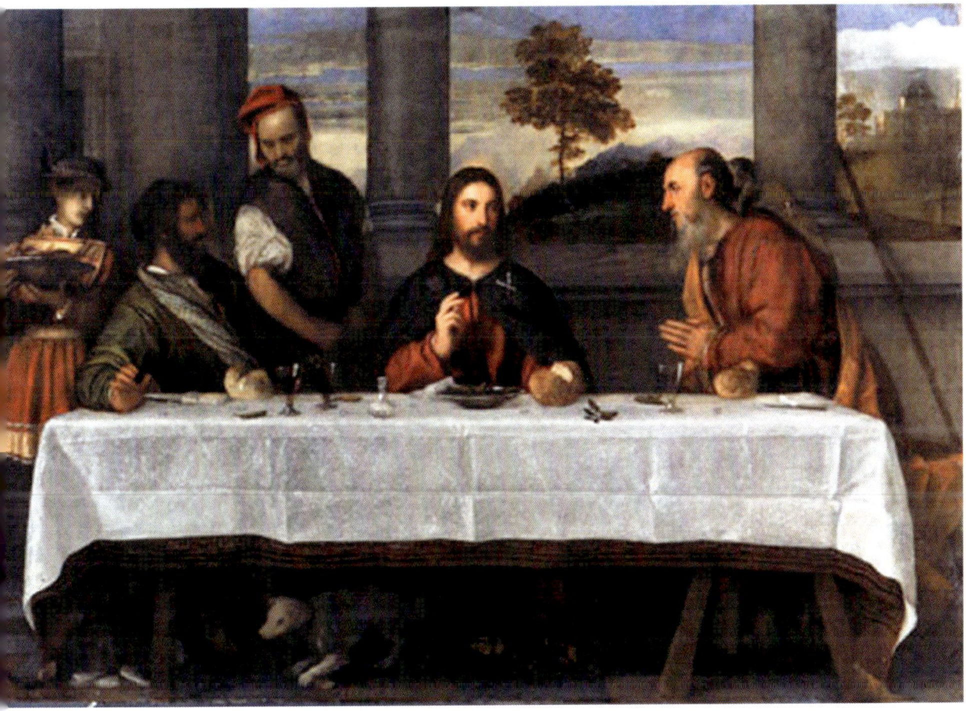

'Supper at Emmaus' by Titian is on loan to the Walker from a private collection. Acknowledgement is made to the Managers of 'the Titian painting for the reproduction of this image.

Queen Elizabeth I: The Pelican Portrait, c. 1574,
attributed to Nicholas Hilliard (1547-1619)

GLASS

My ladies slide my arms into silk sleeves, pull
the corseted back tight, squeeze the breath
from my lungs. They slip ivory
mules on my massaged feet, whiten my face,
pin tight red curls to my own.
Hands powdered, cheeks rouged,
my rings pushed into place.
Silver pelican pinned to my breast,
its wings spread: an embrace to its children,
as my arms are open to my people.

My ladies leave, close the door,
all but Bess. She pulls an empty box
from beneath the bed. None know of this
ethereal dress, its glass bonded in shades
of lilac to deepest iris.
Bess lifts it out, stooping under the weight,
her hands rip on the sharp edges.
We feed my arms into the sleeves,
long like my mother's dresses.
My dress is not studded with sapphires
or laced with gold. It is not a glass of fashion.
It expands to cover the material beneath, glass
becoming liquid for a moment.
The inside is smooth, fragments fitting
perfectly, not a snag in the deep red
silk. It catches the light, throws it
across the room like a church window.
The neck curves to rest
under my chin, the bottom
a bell, balancing on the floor.

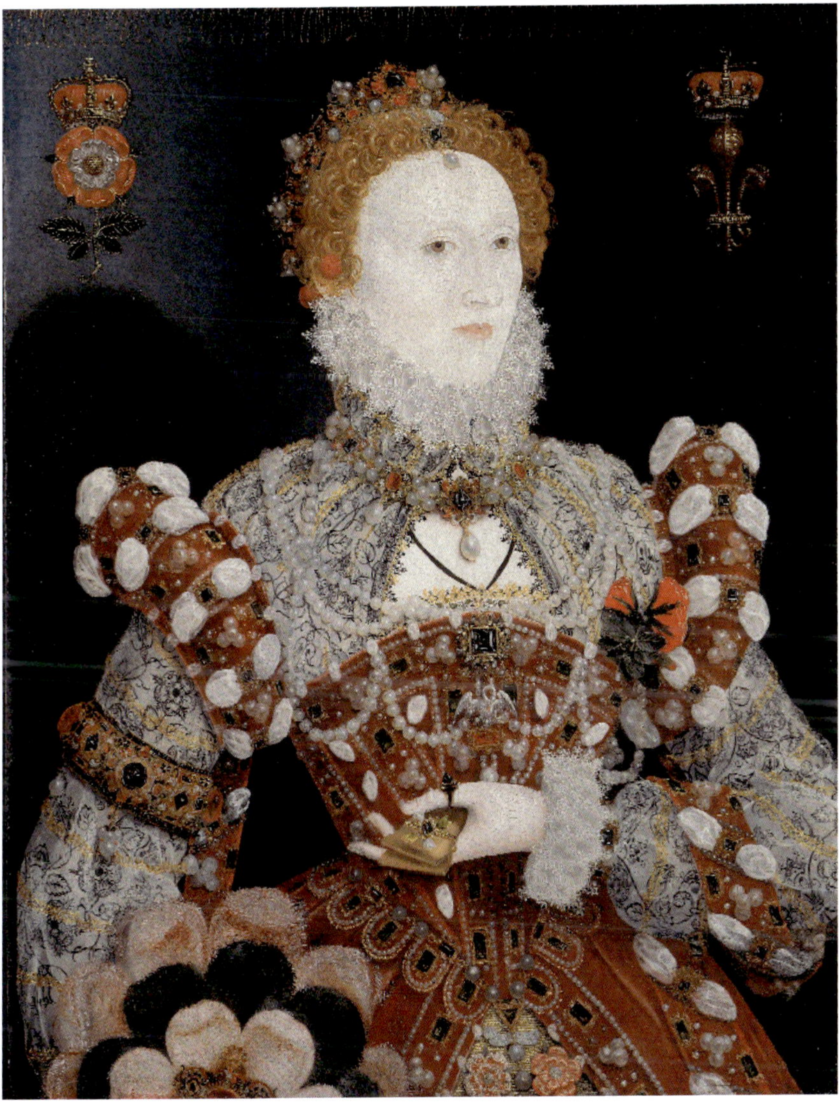

My scarlet and cream gown is darker
beneath amethyst, its lace roses magnified
under the glass only we can see.
Bess ties laces so sharp
they slice her fingers, pulled so tight
I am impenetrable.

Alysa Thomas

Self-portrait as a Young Man, c.1630, Rembrandt van Rijn
(1606-1669)

AN EARLY ATTEMPT IN THE CHANGING ROOM

Look for me
where I learned to look for myself –
in my ring of attempts
in the light of a sinking candle.

A candle?
                    My soul, if you will.
My paintings bear witness to its
harsh affair with the real.
My flesh preferred games and counterfeits.

Counterfeits?
                    My portraits!
The diary I kept in pigments.
This youthful 'me' – one instance –
in a beret and swaggering chain.

The sneer on my lips?
Well, that's Envy spurring Ambition.
The gold of my cheek and chin?
That's the cost of Pretence.

So I played to the glass,
desiring the sweets of applause.
Every morning delivered my face
to a rasher cause:

van Rijn, the actor, the lover,
the courtier, the beggar,
the burgher, the sinner,
the saint, the seducer…

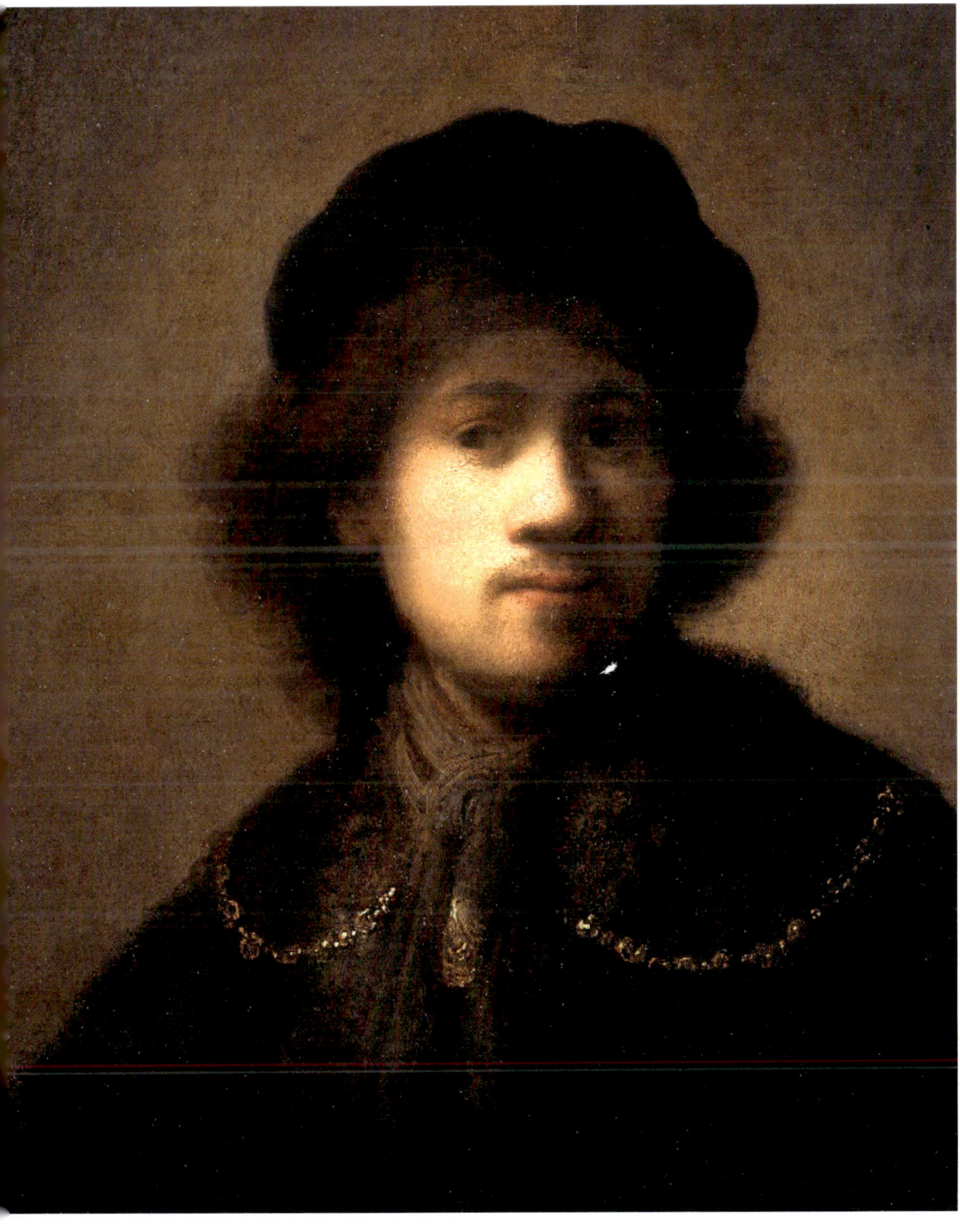

The more lies I told under cover
the truer they were.

For my pictures, whatever my will,
told the truth to my eyes.
My ingenium? God's punishing muscle!
At war with my skill.

With your skill?
Your election by God?

More likely the devil.
My struggles with God
rivalled Jacob's. With the angel.
Even as a young man.
I knew where I stood.

Here was God. Here was Lucifer.
I prayed to them both, damned both,
took what I could.

From Lucifer, light – ochre and lead-white.
A fine brush for elegance – linen and gold.
The wit to paint glory and splendour in firelight.

But from the Lord God, eyes.

And when He handed me eyes,
I knew I'd never escape them.
I shrunk them, I botched them again and again
in the shade of my hair or hat.
I surrounded my forehead with shadows,
wore black and more black.

But my eyes still insisted I judge
myself through them –
myself in the changing room of myself,
myself in Act One on the world's stage,
my root nose, lecherous, cruel, and too thick,
my smooth skin bared for the plague,
myself who would see myself mocked in old age,
poor, unrepentant, disappointed … sick, sick!

'Self-portrait as a young man'.
Ignorant, egotistical, clever young man.
Who could know then
what I'd be in years to come?
Or what eventually did or must happen?

Anne Stevenson

Anne Stevenson notes:
This poem could not have been written without constant recourse to Simon Schama's magnificent study, Rembrandt's Eyes (Allen Lane, Penguin, 1999)

The Betrothal, c. 1640-50, School of Rembrandt

THE BETROTHAL

We pretended at betrothal, for free champagne, the mischief. On one finger I sampled a quarter of a million pounds worth of diamonds set in platinum/white/yellow gold bands. Nobody wants yellow gold right now, but I would take it. I sipped on my champers, not wanting to look greedy, needing to appear nonchalant about fine things the way people with money do. The couple at the next table really was buying the ring and they looked thoroughly casual about it. She should have seemed to love him with a passion, like me, all over him in the way of the coquette, whilst he sat stoic at the seat, easy with this process of acquisition. He should have worn a suit, like my beau, like a real man with a serious matter in hand, not trainers, not a designer woolly, and certainly not rattling his car keys like a toddler. I wanted to make them notice our fervour, our authentic love, because they were going to leave with the little bag, barely scooping bubbles from the thin glass. I wanted to finish their champagne for them. I wondered if a cheeky member of staff would do that – it must be a long day watching love waltz in and out of the door, bringing the cold in with it. A marriage should not be based on illusion, but it is defined by the effort you are prepared to make. I called my beau Mr. D in front of the saleswoman, affecting a sugar-daddy dynamic (though he exceeds my age by a mere three years). I wriggled into the cuddle of his arm, and because he loves me, and a free drink, he played straight guy to my delighted dolly. When I looked away, the saleswoman slipped him a card detailing the price and description of my favourite pieces and he slid it inside his jacket with the discretion of a secret agent, getting into role himself, confident now the game was a success. Outside, a few steps down the street, we giggled, kissed, smoked a roll-up, said we'd get married today if we had the money, if we had a ring. Then we saw it in the gutter; the little bag from the shop, it must have fallen as they swanked off in their bubble of wealth. We looked inside the bag but it was empty, nothing more than a sweetie wrapper. I would have kept the packaging too.

Deborah Marie Morgan

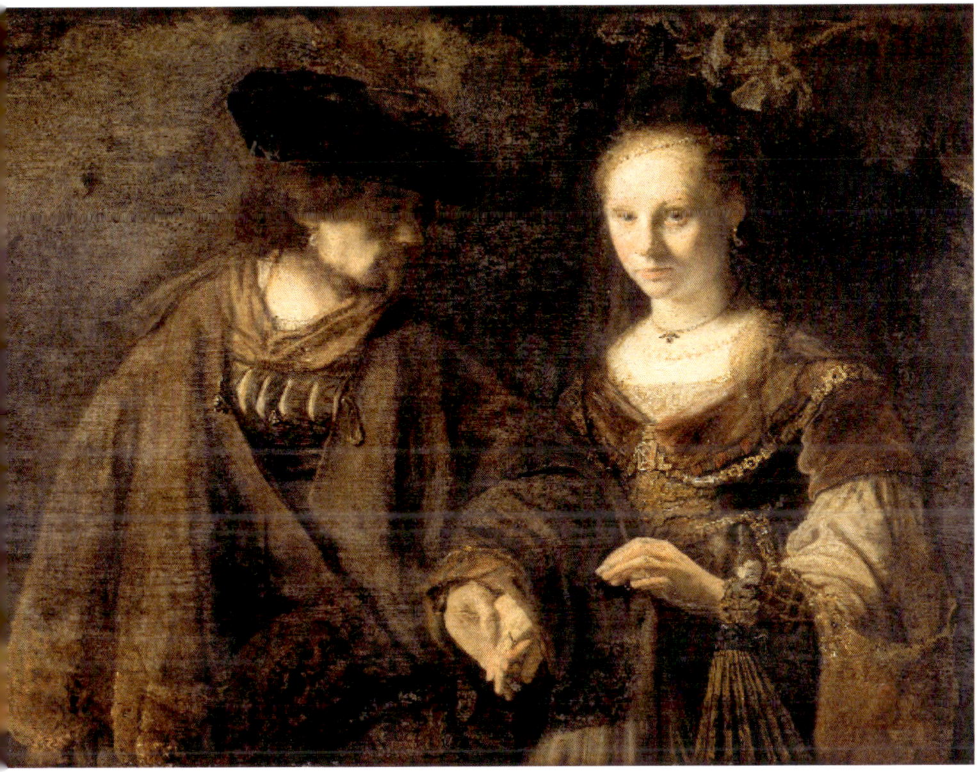

Fleetwood Hesketh, 1769, Joseph Wright of Derby (1734-97)

FLEETWOOD: A MINI PERIOD DRAMA

FLEETWOOD *poses.*
HOLLY *giggles.*
JOSEPH *dabs his brush on his palette.*

FLEETWOOD You don't mind if she stays awhile Mister Wright. You behave yourself Holly.

HOLLY He's s bad one Mister Wright. I calls him my 'bad Harry'.

FLEETWOOD You sit over there.

HOLLY If I sit over there I won't be in the picture.

JOSEPH *considers his palette. The possibilities of Holly's dirty apron over her magenta frock, and the golden curls tumbling down her pearly skin are daunting and exciting.*
HOLLY *tweaks her lover's cheek and grins at* JOSEPH.
JOSEPH *notices a missing tooth behind the tip of her wide smile. He dips his brush in hunting red.*

FLEETWOOD Holly you can't. This is a portrait for the future, it's going to hang in the house.

HOLLY Like your Dad. An' his dad. But Mister Wright didn't paint them. (*Beat*) I seen a painting. It's a picture of one of them men what works in the dye factory an' his hands is all blue.

JOSEPH *dabs his brush on his palette and squints at Fleetwood.*

Dymphna Callery

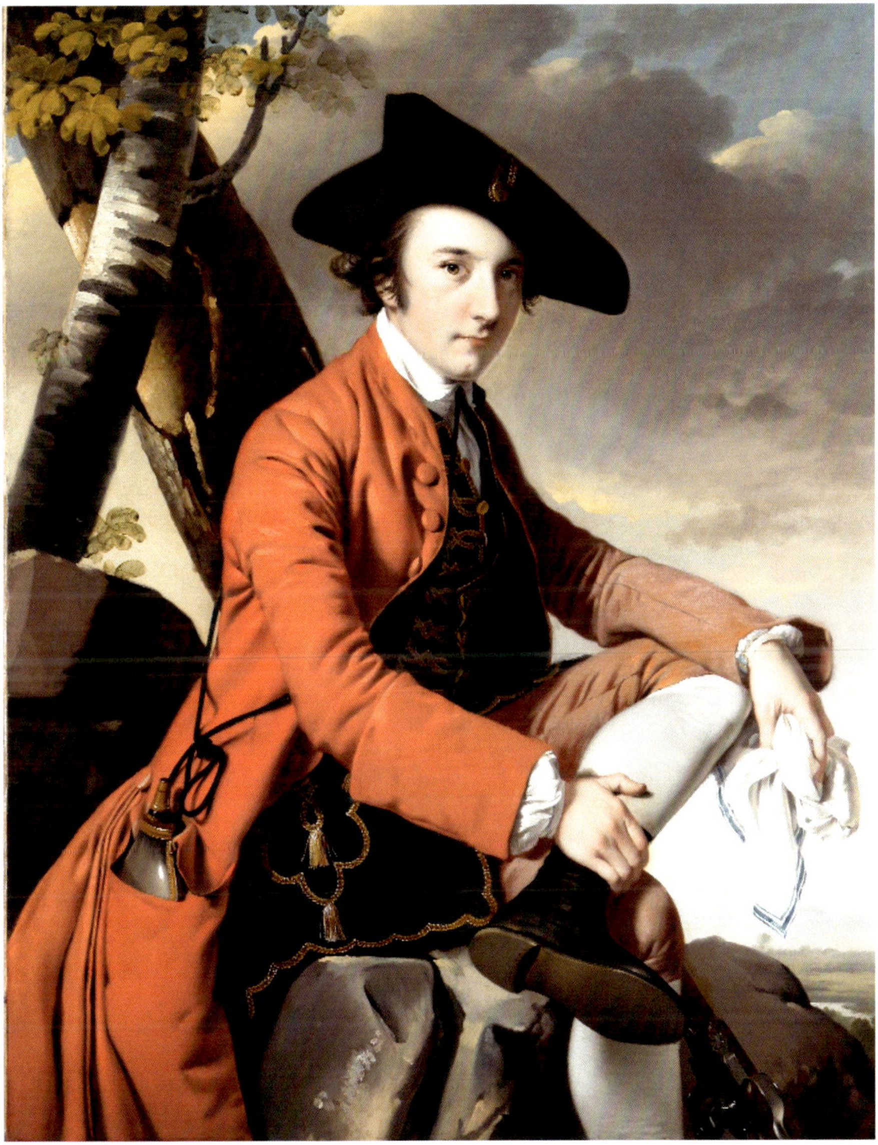

Horse frightened by a lion, 1770, George Stubbs, (1724-1806)

HORSE FRIGHTENED BY A LION

From out of fine weather comes triangular thought
a puzzle on the wind, a mistake of hooves

edging a river bank. The fine head looks down
a guesswork of cloud

unmasked haunches so clearly white
rear to heartstop - breath.

Sound reverberates from trees
hiding their pity in shallows.

The stink is fear, a sense of knowing
this is *the* day

when the reaches of being will snap
as sure as harpstring in a leonine face.

Cynthia Kitchen

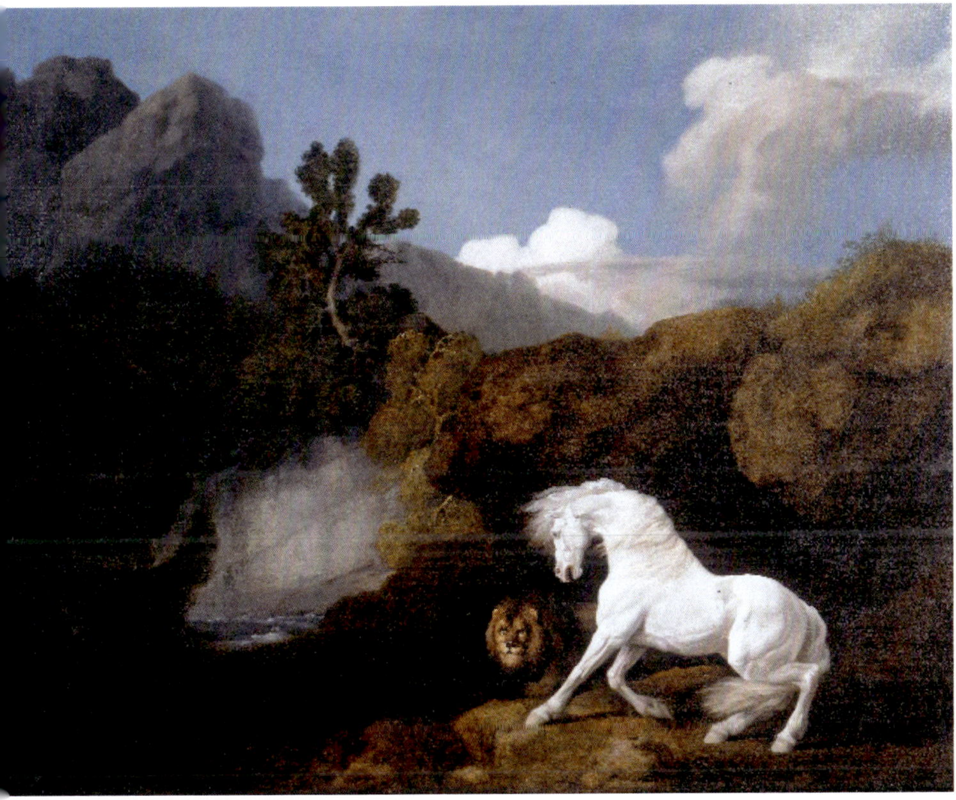

The Annual Girandola at the Castel Sant'Angelo, Rome, 1775-76,
Joseph Wright of Derby (1734-1797)

FIREWORKS

Flying splinters of flame
Shooting from the Girandola
Light the Roman sky,
Casting a golden shroud,
Enveloping the Vatican.

Easter is here.
With joyous shouts the people
Celebrate the ascension of Christ,
He who gives their lives focus
For living, dying, rising.

Eveline Paulson

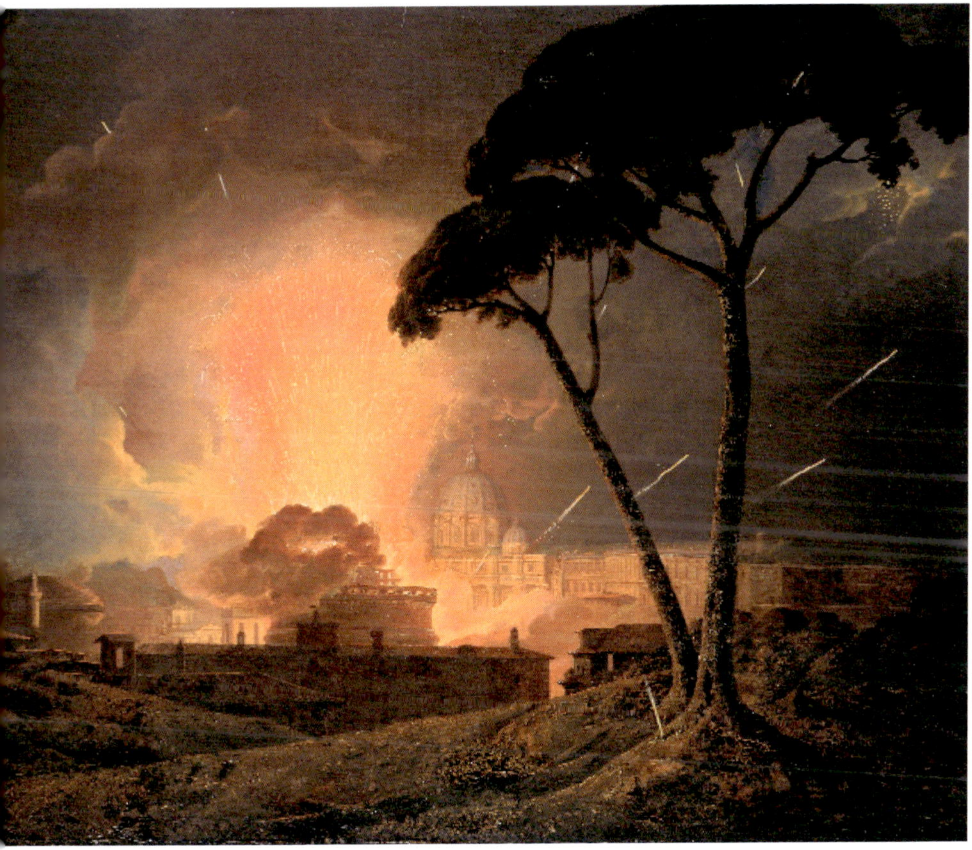

Interior of a Foundry, with Visitors, 1789, Léonard Defrance (1735-1805)

VISITING THE IRON FOUNDRY

The woman stands in the furnace glare, her face
Inscrutable. The lackey holds her lap dog
At her side. The frothing fine white swathes
About her neck, and headdress too, she thinks,
Are flecked with black already. Why has he brought
Her here, to all this stinking heat and grime?
The sweating labourers wield their globes of iron,
Glowing, molten, spilling incandescence
Across the stone-flagged floor, hoisting the ore
So seeming clumsily; but really dexterous.
She can see that. Those handles two yards long!
She'd like to see her woman manage kitchen
Tools that length. Gloveless, she holds her fan
Still folded. Useless here! He catches at her arm
In all this roar and clang and din to tell
Some detail, newly gleaned from the foundry man.
In the flickering light he seems to flicker, too,
Diminished by the stalwart men who work
All day in this, his Hades. Did he hope
To impress her with his power? He's failed. She sees
The humorous glint in one worker's eyes, his hand
On the other's shoulder, curling lips at his ear.
They don't belong here, she and this man who courts
Her. Though he may own this Devil's world he's dwarfed
By the skills and sinews of the men who serve
The foundry's maw and roar. He ought instead
To have shown her around his offices, or
The new planned garden at his country house.
She'll marry him, of course. He's rich and has
Some standing in the prosperous town, although
He's neither titled, nor a gentleman of leisure.

Pat Fearon

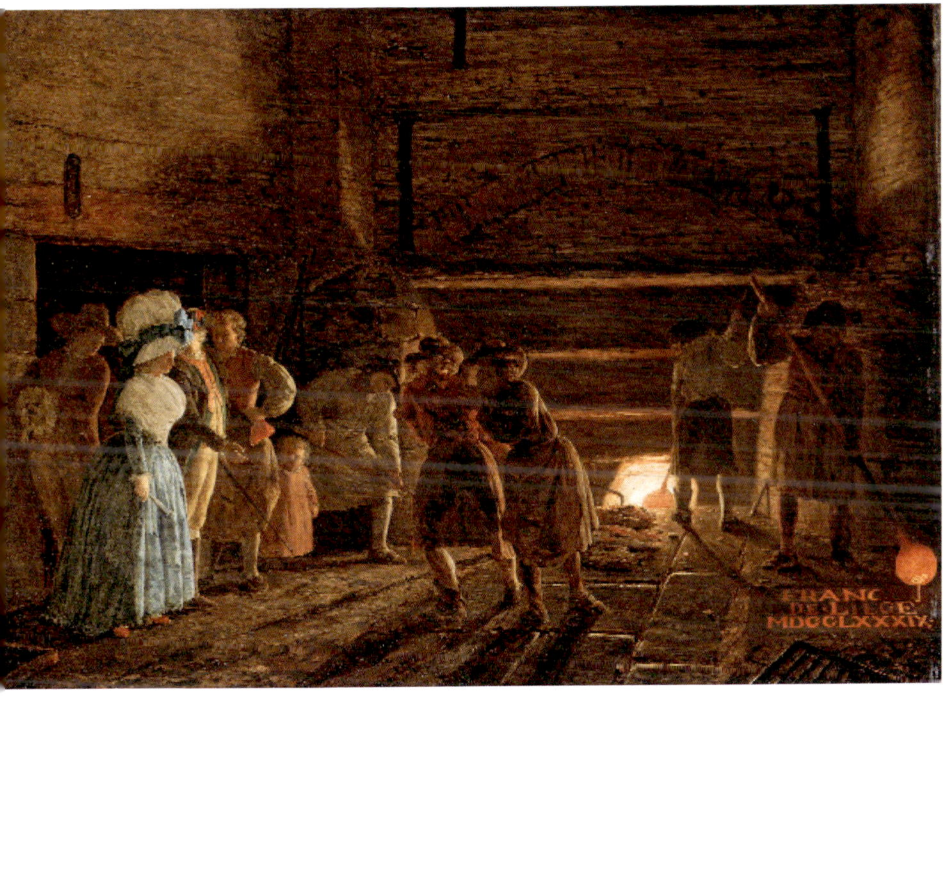
FRANC
MDCCLXXXIX

Linlithgow Palace, 1807, Joseph Mallord William Turner (1775-1851)

LINLITHGOW PALACE

Your eyes bring you back to the centre.
Bathers, exposed, all bare in ice-fresh water
and sandy loch-bank light.
Branches catch, point out, and hold their clothes.

Dead tree-trunks reach up
to ruins of an ancient, heat-hazed
and loch-moated royal palace.
Linlithgow holds its crown high,
twice fire-torn but still standing,
defiant, rebuilt but roofless.
Sheep share its steep secrets
where many Stewart kings rested, lived.
Queens, reflecting, have looked down
from the turrets and dizzying defences.
Once chambers and floors were hem-swept;
now the winds are free
to find their way through stone.
Distance recedes into ruins
set in a peel, hammered by Edward 1.

The two bathers lift out or drop
into cool currents a naked figure;
these nymphs cavort. Their laughter
before or after the splash, is gathered,
stilled, painted. Their lives long gone,
like generations between the palace walls,
their moment faded yet framed. A memory
that will never be ruined.

Ceri Courtenay

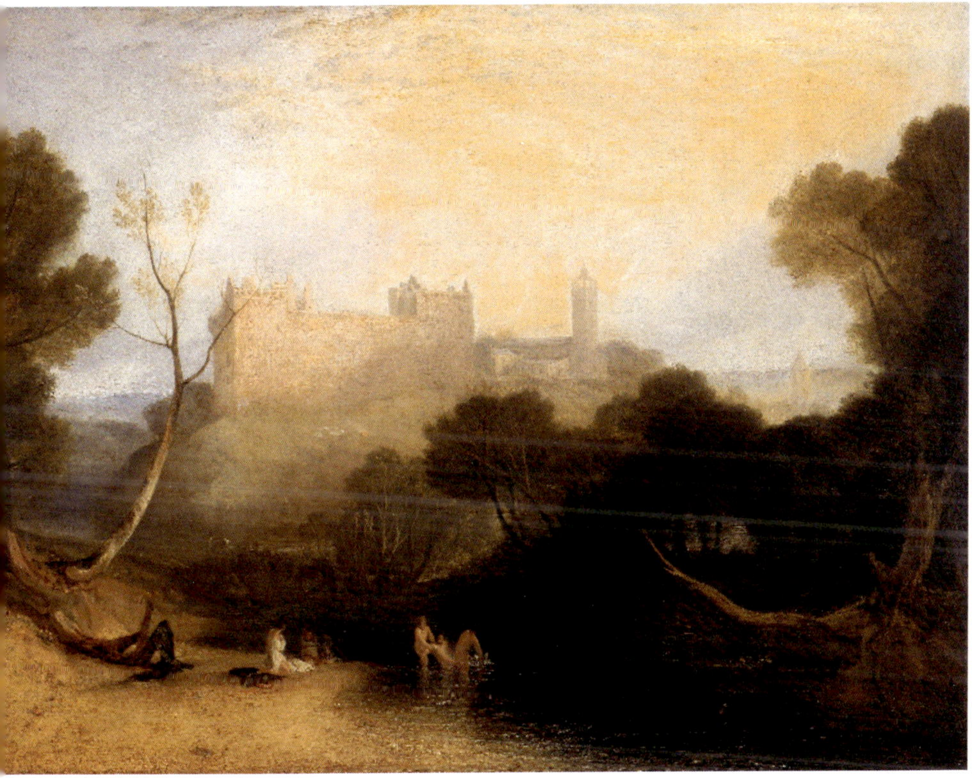

The Ruins of Holyrood Chapel, c.1824, Louis Daguerre (1787-1851)

THE RUINS OF HOLYROOD CHAPEL

1.

Misty twilight dawn
fights long shadows
for supremacy of the chapel.

The ruined stones
and cracked flags
heave with life,
ferns and flowers
sway like hair and feathers.

The altar is smooth –
since the day it was made
it gives the birds
and wild creatures
a place to pray to their gods.

The chess king watches
his palace come to life.

2. The Chess King

It's quiet in here.
The early morning sounds
die before they reach the walls.
A slice of dawn light
accentuates the darkness,
making it more whole,
more black.

The arched window lets me
see a moment of forest
and mountain.
A picture with edges
and nothing beyond but sky.

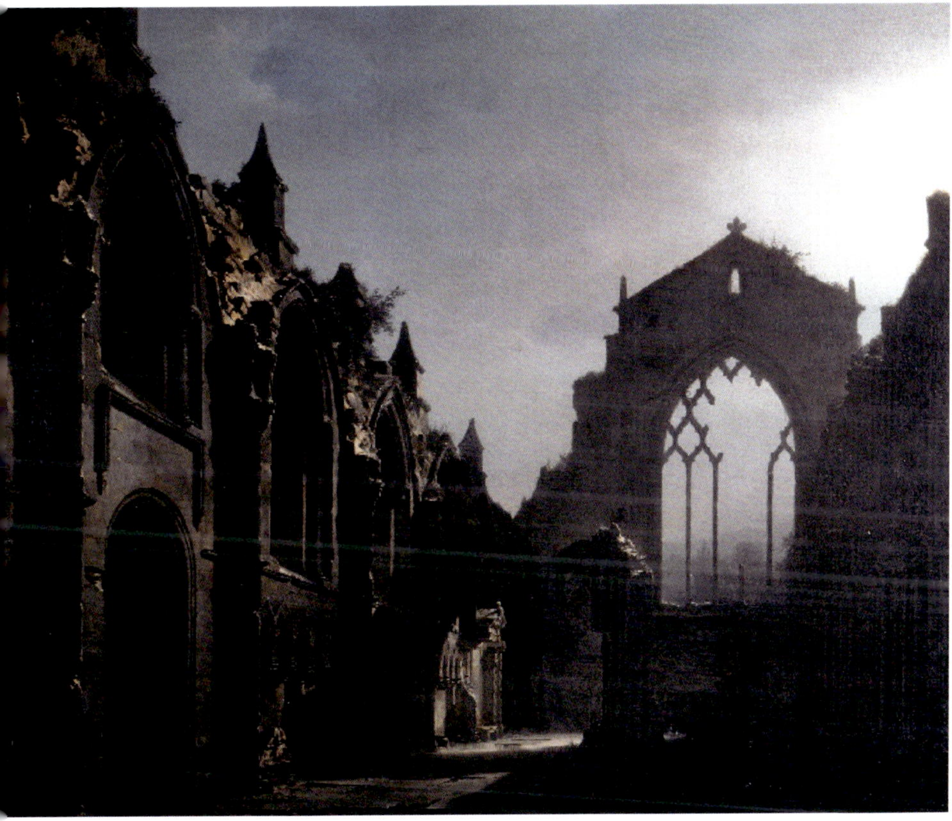

It’s quiet in here,
ghosts make no sounds
as they tread the cold, hard
broken ground.
I watch them melt
in the slice of sunlight,
gone before I can say
hello.

Elaine Wilson

Returning from the Haunts of the Seafowl, c.1833, William Collins (1788-1847)

SEA CLIFF, BIRDS AND CHILDREN

We spin out over the pit, slip on the grass, if we are not careful. Balance
the easel two hundred feet above the sand, hard below, peopled by mites, unaware.
The wind chimes in the grasses, whips up eddies in the empty air.

Above us, two boys whoop, sticks wheeling, no foretaste of plunging
down the rocks' spines on to that killing floor. Up here, life is adrenaline
and blood lust, searching for eggs among the ledges, the birds' screams.

They mill, yelling, distressed, 'Kitti-wake, kitti-wake, keep away!'
plundered, fruitless, they circle, wings winnowing, lament their young.
A third boy, safer, urges his friends, 'This way, over here!' The dog
alone is awed by the drop, stands taut and anxious on the edge.

Below, through air made vertiginous, like funnels, a vista of sea,
creaming the sand, leaping, too far to hear; as ever uncaring
of youth and excitement, of loss, of damage, impending destruction.

Susan Craggs

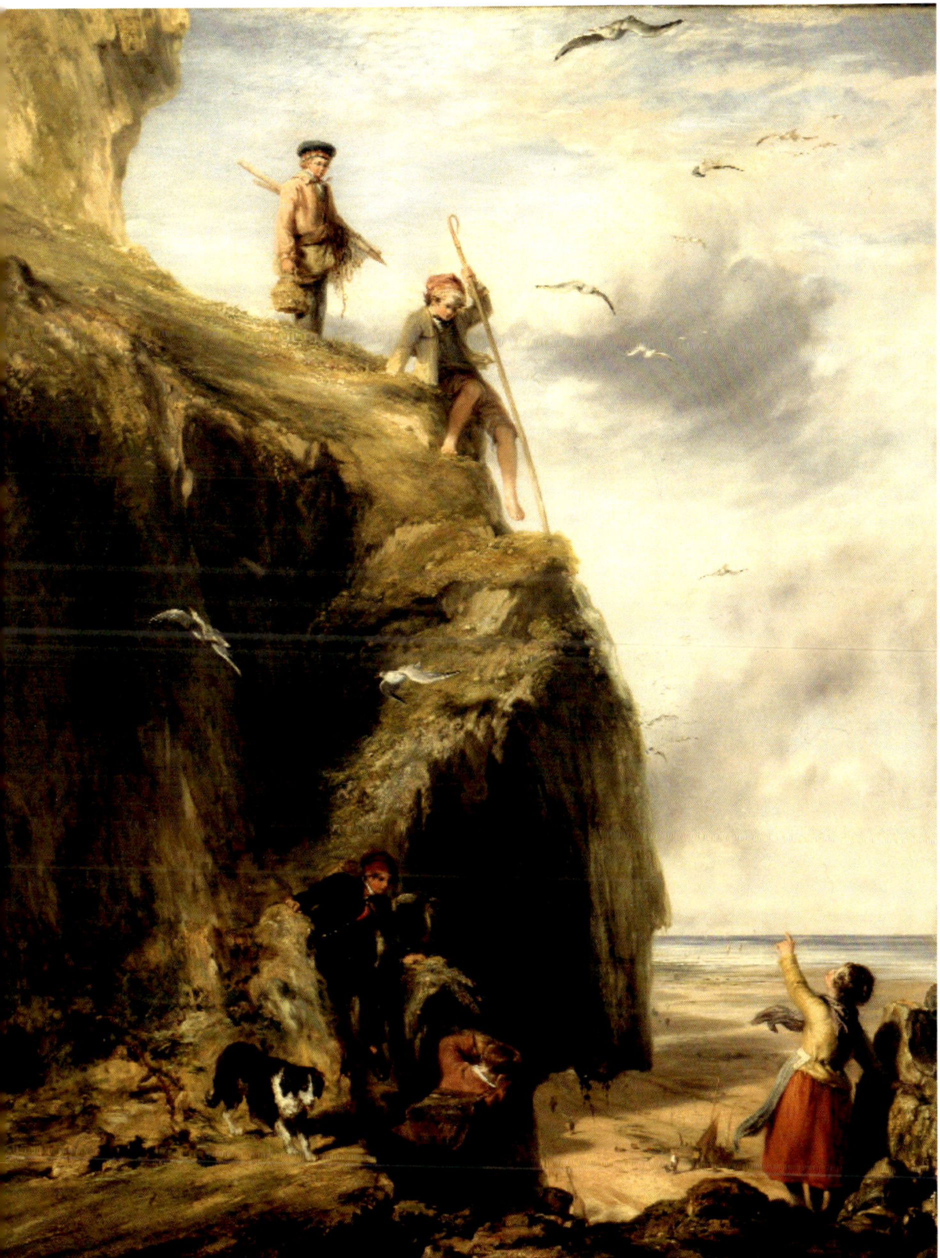

The Eve of the Battle of Edgehill, 1642, 1845, Charles Landseer (1799-1879)

AFTER EDGEHILL, 1642

1. Villagers report *The Late Apparitions*

A December Saturday, star-clear,
at Kineton. Three months since the battle,
the village collects itself – Christmas
perhaps a demarcation, a control
in the blood-letting. Yet on the ridge
of Edge Hill, the night resounds,
armies grinding one against the other
re-enacting the action, re-dying the deaths.

Shepherds hear trumpets, drums –
expect a visitation of holy kings with retinues.
Instead, the spectral soldiers strike,
icy night skies crack with cries,
steel clashing and the sput of muskets.
A knot of Kineton men watch, witness;
Samuel Marshall, the Minister, says
the Devil's apparitions seize the dead.

2. A Ghost Speaks

I am unplanted, my world this waste –
the heath where bone was split, undressed of flesh,
where arteries unleashed their flood, the colour
of death. What is the colour of honour? The blue
in which we dissolve into air? The white of ashes?
Can I be woven into the braids of her hair, my lady,
or exist in the quick of my son's fingernails?
I, who carried the Standard, once drove the plough,
turning up earth, the harvest of worms. Now I envy
the seeds in the furrow, their dark cradle.
My blood is this Midlands field, this hacked hedgerow
where I lie, hearing the drumbeat of the dead,
corpses strewn rotting, graveless.

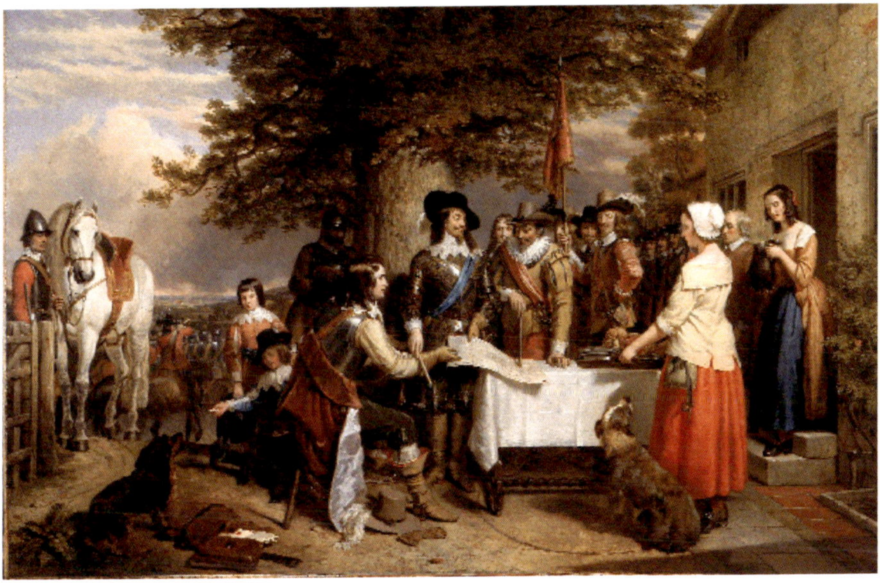

I glide up and down these rows of human manure,
the faces of soldiers like fallen cameos.
Here is Sir Edmund Verney, Thomas Transome –
they look skywards, lolling near my own wistful face.
Sir Edmund is grimacing slightly as he did in life,
Thomas Transome's skull a broken eggshell.

The brittle linnet flies from me. Dry leaves relinquish
their hold on twigs. A hare sits motionless, watching,
listening to last groans forever in the wind.
I see a troop of Horse on the skyline – Parliament's.
They charge our pikemen; now they vanish
like moving cloud-shadows across the field.
I cannot follow the clouds; I am chained to my carcass
hovering, as others are, above their unburied selves.

3. A Dragoon observes Colonel Cromwell

Like a falcon from the gauntlet, he throws off these deaths.
He tells us *Smile out to God in Praise*, for his is the sword
of the Lord. I see his horse, piebald with blood.

Gladys Mary Coles

The Tinted Venus, c.1851-1856, John Gibson (1791-1866)

VENUS

Elegant drapery, warm ivory tinted flesh,
blonde hair coiled under a net of blue and gold;
your delicate hand holds the golden apple –
a Greek inscription, 'To the most beautiful'.

Medici Venus – Aphrodite, Goddess of Love.
Artistically a sensation,
your debut divided opinion, confounded critics.
A commanding entry into the Victorian Age.

Fame seems a heavy burden,
trapped in your temple of columns and glass.
Gazing out, elegance surrounds you –
Flora, Cupid, Pysche at the well.

Does your essence long to be free?
Perhaps as a Botticelli Venus
silently compelling us forward
reaching out across the millenia.
Against a sea of cobalt blue
she reclines languidly, a pearl in her shell.
As a Patron goddess of Pompeii
once she was trapped in her tomb of ash.
Now she is free and gazes from her frescoed wall.

Maybe one day our tinted Venus also will escape.

Muriel Cordon

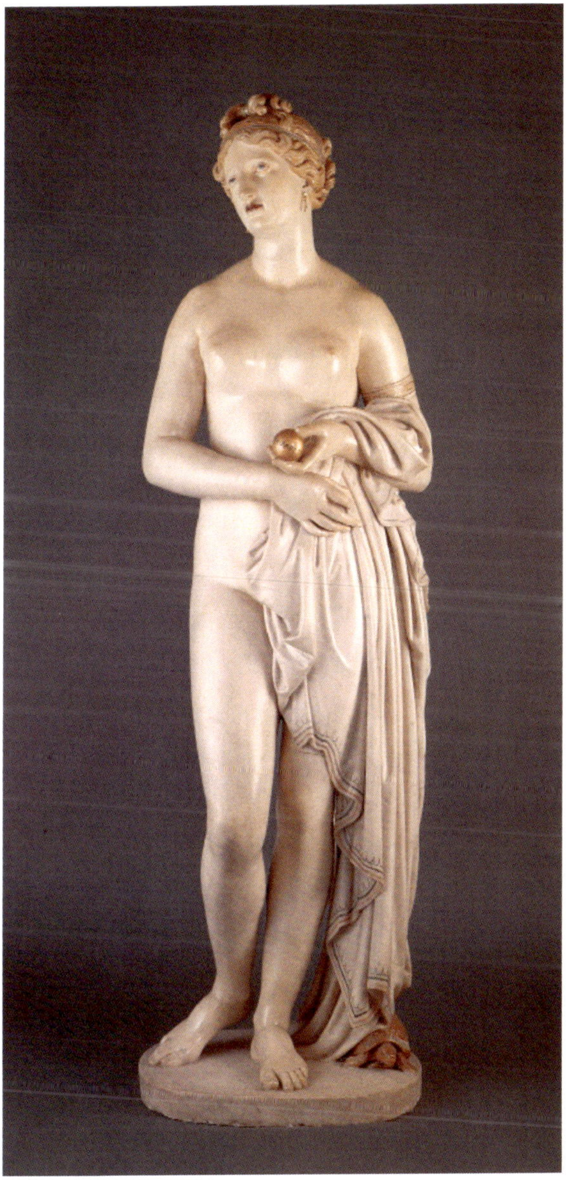

The Dragon's Den, c.1854, James Campbell (1828-1893)

THE DRAGON'S DEN

I wish I could step into this painting.
Live in a world of shimmering colour.
Some of the leaves shine like lapis,
They appear to be crafted from crystal
As though some creature actually
Carved a place
And scattered emerald shavings
Over the ground,
Then draped green silk around
Trunks of trees,
Blew gold dust over rocks,
Gilding them.

As though some creature
Made its own paradise
And secreted itself away,
Never again to be seen.

Jane Batty

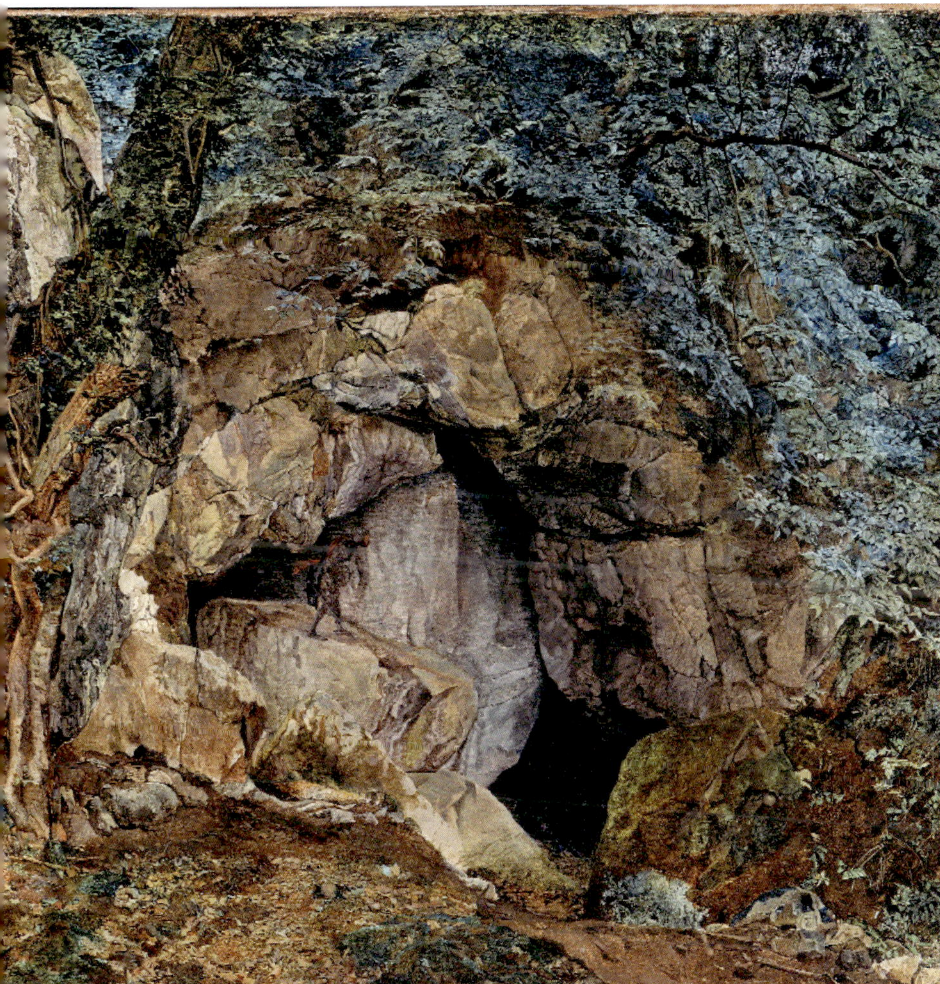

The Eve of St. Agnes, c.1847-57, William Holman Hunt (1827-1910)

TWO MEN AND A DOG

JK I was young. In fact, I have always been young.
But a young poet deviates. He needs to be understood.
So I gave all the clues I could: the exact
Date; a very cold winter; St. Agnes'
Story; stressed chill and old age
At both sides of the poem, the triptych
Of freezing owl, and storm and coffin-worm,
Between both a feast for epicures,
And Madeleine warm, undressed,
Porphyro, ethereal, flushed, like a throbbing star –
You follow, don't you? The furnace
At the heart of the rose. But this numbskull
Misses the elegant candies, the tastes, aromas,
The iridescence (O the lovely senses,
The lovely words). They miss their chances,
These daubers. I knew Haydon and Severn;
I would have shown them how it should be.

HH Mine is the subtle version. That's why
I left out all the vapid obvious stuff.
See how he flaunts the spices, delicatessen,
Bosoms, trumpets – not my scene at all.
En plein air is my favourite. I am *not*
A camera. The discriminating eye
Rejects the obvious, the flat. See what I made
Of the porter, splayed along the foreground
(Keats merely gives him a capital P),
I made him a welter of perspectives.
As for the lovers: Keats has them vague
I have them dressed and ready for the road.
Note all the *possible* things: the door might creak,
The dog might bark, the revellers wake –
These are the delicacies paint alone contrives,
Not the rude boorishness of poetry.
I'm sad he's dead. He could have learned from me.

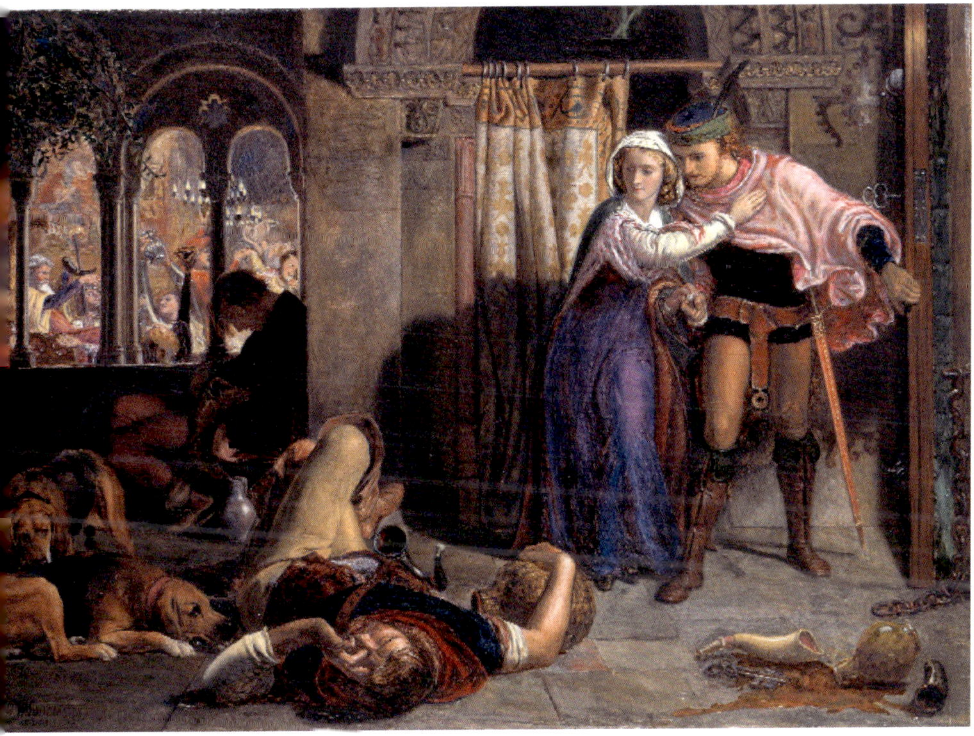

DOG Both got it wrong. You have to feel for dogs
Before you paint or write them. I, the dog,
Recognise the inmates. What does a dog do?
Silently wag his tail, of course. Neither of them
Got that.
And, incidentally,
How many dogs are there supposed to be?

U. A. Fanthorpe

Edward Lear, 1857, *William Holman Hunt* (*1827-1910*)

A MIDDLE-AGED MAN FROM HIGHGATE

A middle-aged man from Highgate
whose pupils unusually dilate ...
milkily, he surfaces

beginning to gaze above our heads
like our father with a yet unfinished secret.
His chin is where

his surprisingly famous hair
and all enterprising colour is:
a turf-lit mountainside

that will freckle at times
with the flat-out shadows
of dolphin, wolf, and tumbling Rhamphorhynchus.

John Redmond

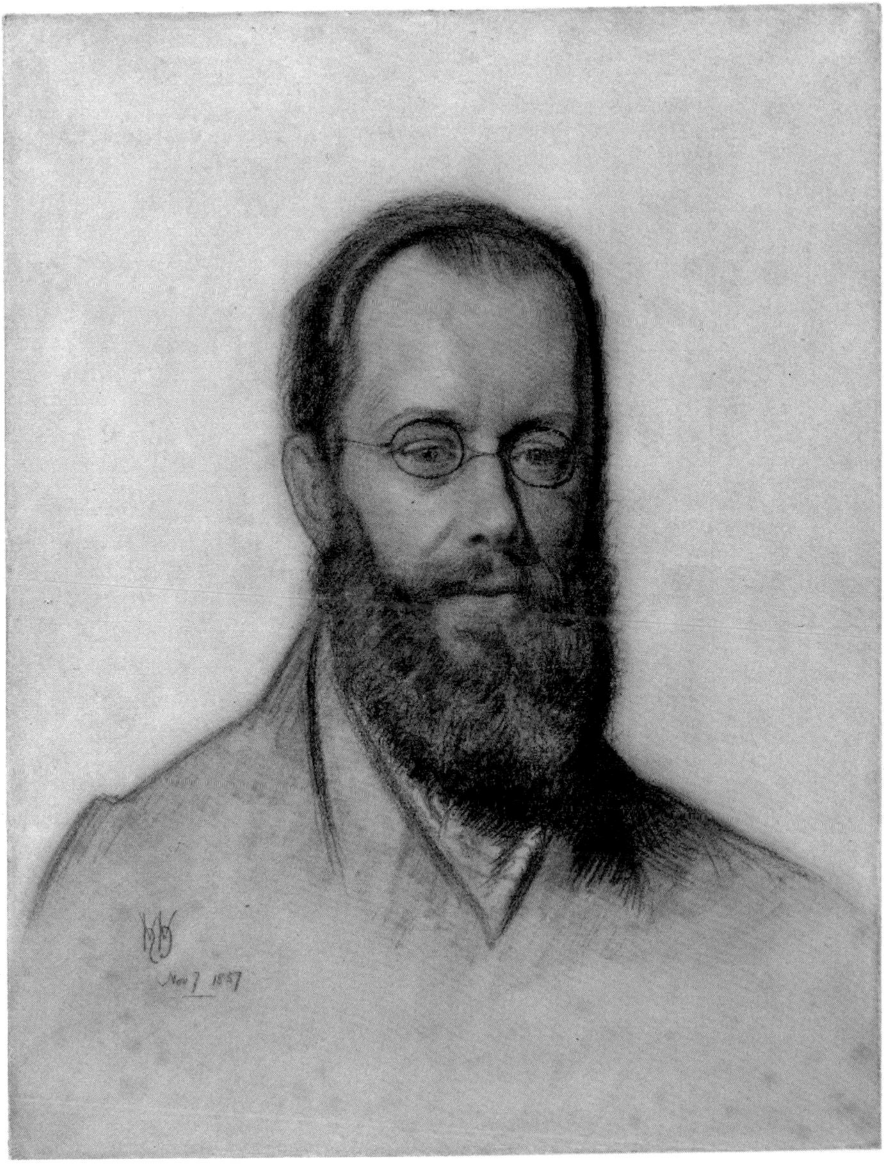
Nov 7 1857

The Murder, c.1867, Paul Cézanne (1839-1906)

THE MURDER

O murderer quiet Cézanne, angry shy and rude

kill yourself and pray the forms will shatter
in binocular vision and parallax silvery night.

In Paris Camille lies dying in the gutter. A guilty
plea from the dock: the trial of *Thérèse Raquin.*

This murder was the true creation, the painting a doodle
from the chthonic gods: the heavy dawn of a fresher art,

the cubical fruit of a new Provence. Light of Pontoise,
          Auvers and Mont Sainte Victoire.

Astonished by your apples (the fruit of an innocent man,
          O murderer quiet Cézanne),

the gutter shines and the bitter monsters leave.

Now wait a century for the telephoto majesty,
the frame sublime of Kurosawa's flickering light.

Woody Allen, even, will cite your incredible apples and pears –
in *Manhattan* – as one of several reasons to live.

O murderer quiet Cézanne, release this blunt troll of sex

in thick paint and black pain to the pastoral idyll
               of bruised cloud and present flesh.

O murderer quiet Cézanne, let these dark shades
          bathe you in the tougher glow of love.

Ade Jackson

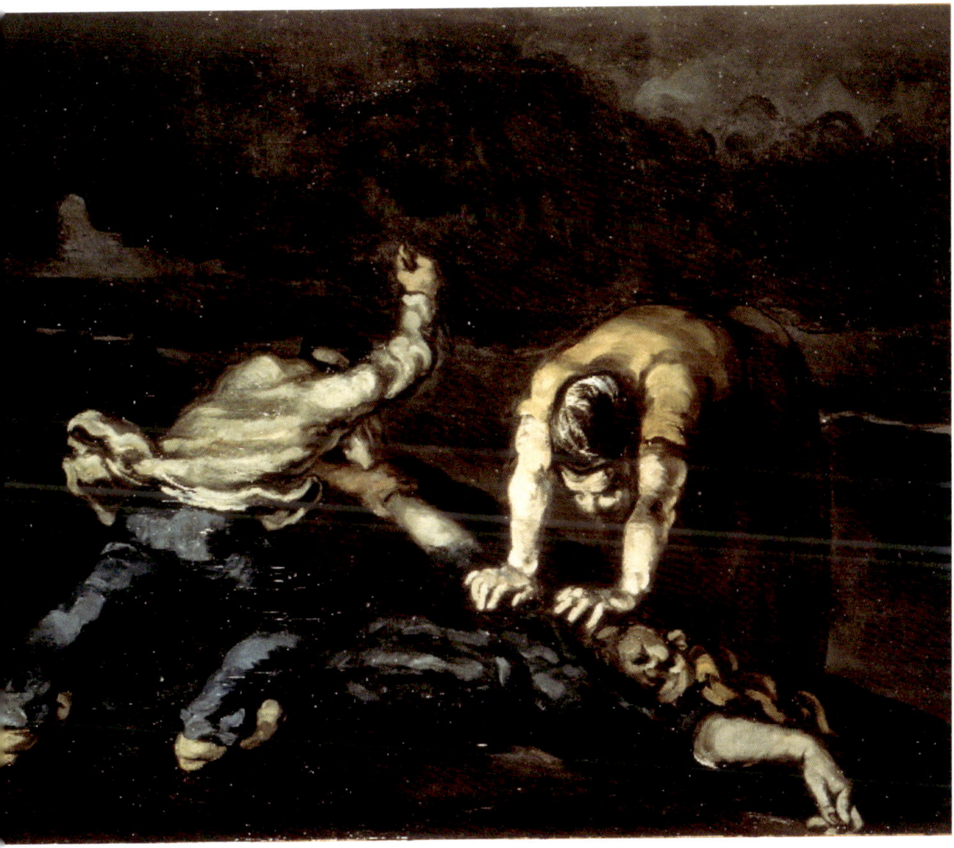

Jane Morris, c.1870, Dante Gabriel Rossetti (1828-82)

JANE'S BAD BACK

Odd to think
she'll be hung in a frame,
though it already feels
like her back's on a hook

and skin's been split
by a ten inch spike
that juts from the gallery wall.

She must sit still
though she can't sit straight,
                                        her height
tucked up so her spine
is a long throb of root
probing through peat
where the bones of an old woman
wait.

But she knows he won't paint this;
he'd rather focus
on the sofa or the softer
angles of lips and hair.

Janette Stowell

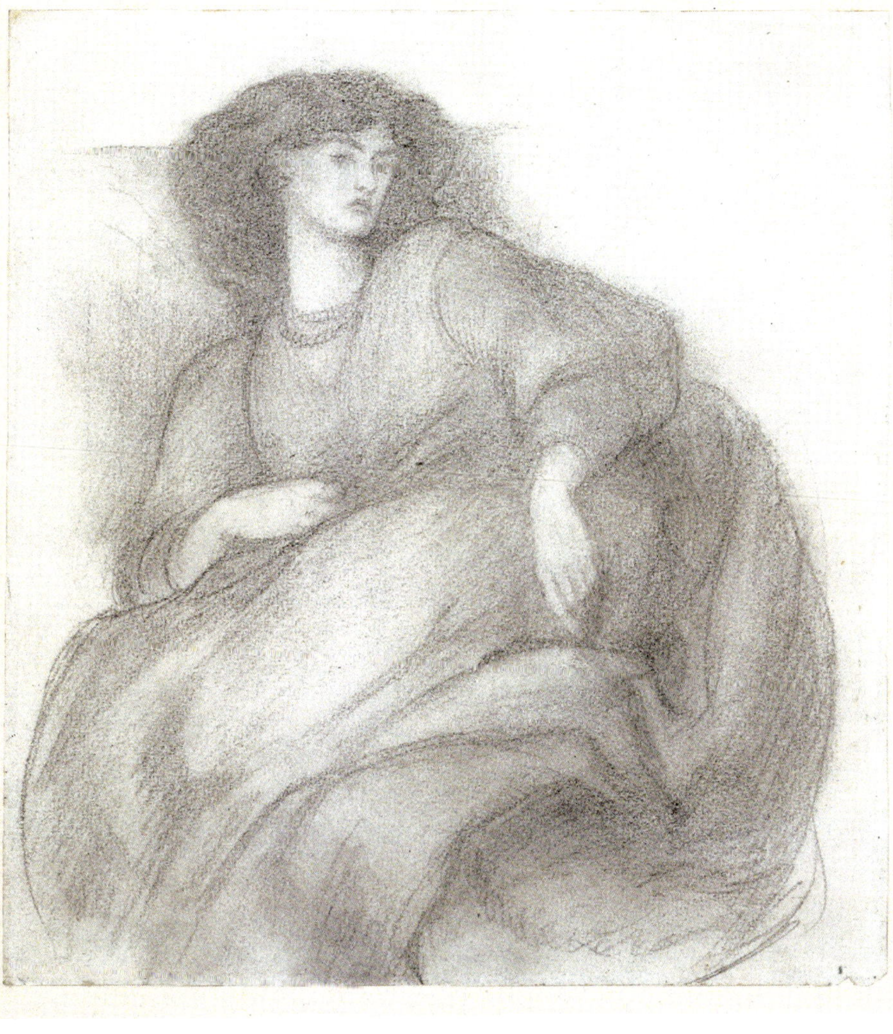

Martyr of Solway, 1871, John Everett Millais (1829-98)

MARTYR OF SOLWAY

I might have had bairns of my own.
Wind whips my breasts, skirt: a lass
Exposed to all. Its raw breath
Sears my nostrils with salt. Waves
Roll nearer, faster, tolling my end.
I am not afraid of death. Lord,
You are my shield, my glory! Chains
Chafe my arms, rasping the flesh –
I might have had bairns of my own!
I am hoarse with singing, not seeing
How many scoff, mock me.
My will is set. Seek not falsehood!
Auld Meg, brave saint, goes before.
Only mother's weeping stings,
Stabs heart, ear with her pleading…
I might have had bairns of my own.
My skirt's sopped, my feet drowned
In the shallows. Spray, cleanse me
Of sin! I brace for sea's cold
Enfolding… In your wings, O Lord,
I take refuge, sing your praises ever, ever –
Ah! I might have had bairns of my own!

Rosemary Doman

The 'Martyr of Solway' was Margaret Wilson, a member of the Free Church, who in 1685 refused to recognise the established Church of Scotland. She was condemned to death by drowning, chained to the rocks in Solway Firth.

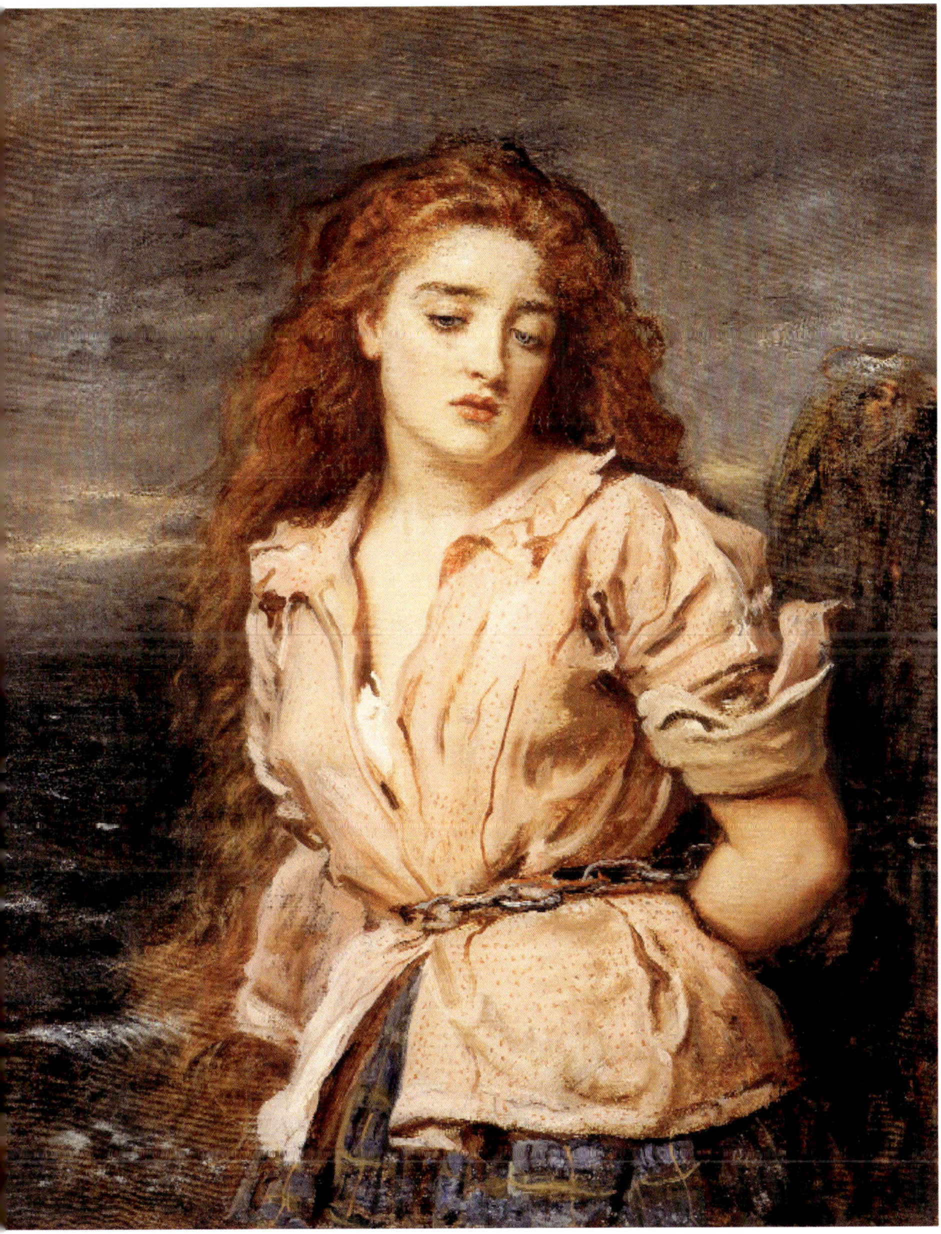

Portrait of Catherine Smith Gill and two of her children, c.1877,
James Tissot (1836-1902)

FLOUNCE

You can see he doesn't care how *I* look, what *I'm* doing.
He only has eyes for Mama, the French *fou.*
So here I am, sitting next to namby-pamby Robby
in white frills and butter-wouldn't-melt smirk.
I've got blue bows – yuk – with black stockings. I refused
to wear all white.

We're shut inside the stuffy drawing room
on a hot afternoon in August. I could be playing
on the lawn, climbing the elm tree, throwing
a ball for little Scrap – he's on the sofa too –
but I'm stuck here, glaring at Monsieur.
How he primps and preens, cocks his head
now this side, now that; steps back, brandishes his brush –
ah, Madame, c'est parfait, alors ...comme ça –
formidable.

As for *maman*. She's ...happy, shiny; she
just doesn't care; she glows, she smiles. I'm not there.
I hate them. I wish
Papa would come home soon.

Margaret Gleave

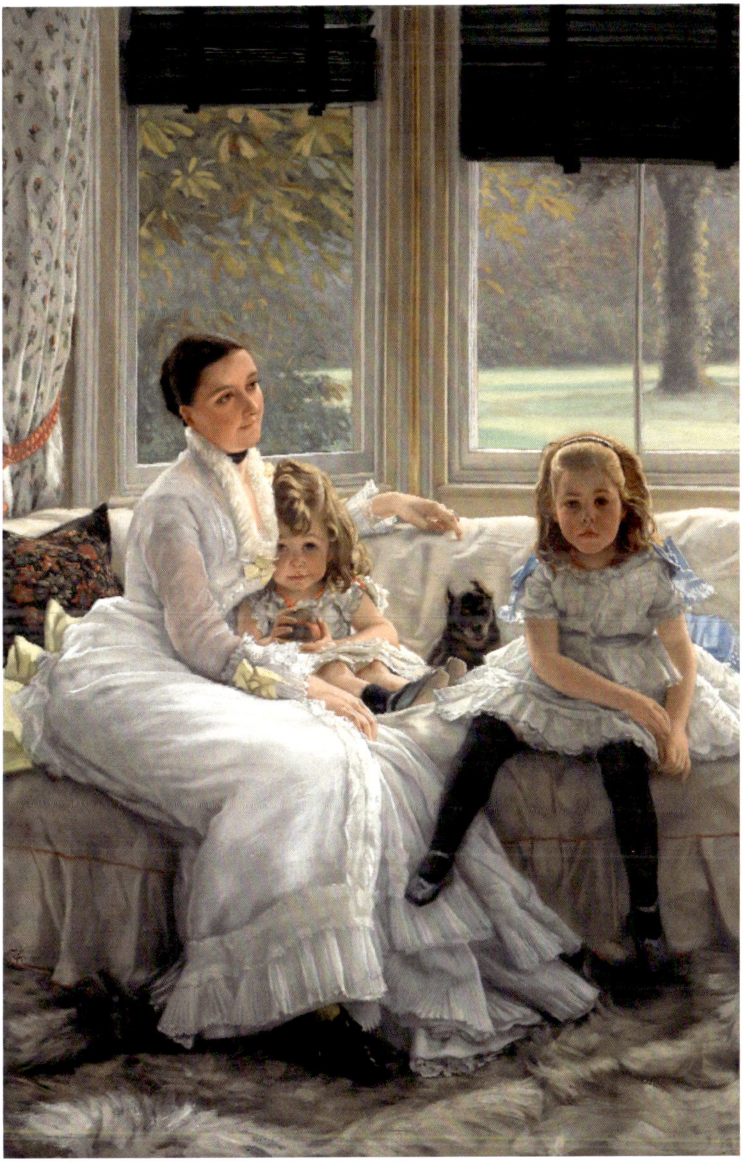

And when did you last see your father? 1878,
William Frederick Yeames (1835-1918)

'And when did you last see your father?'
Asked the boy. The officer leaned forward bemused:
'Don't get all hoity-toity with me
We roundheads are not easily amused.

You stand there before me, dressed all in blue
May I put the same question politely to you?'
'You may not,' said the boy, 'do you think me a fool?'
Then he smiled and bowed, and stepped down from the stool.

Roger McGough

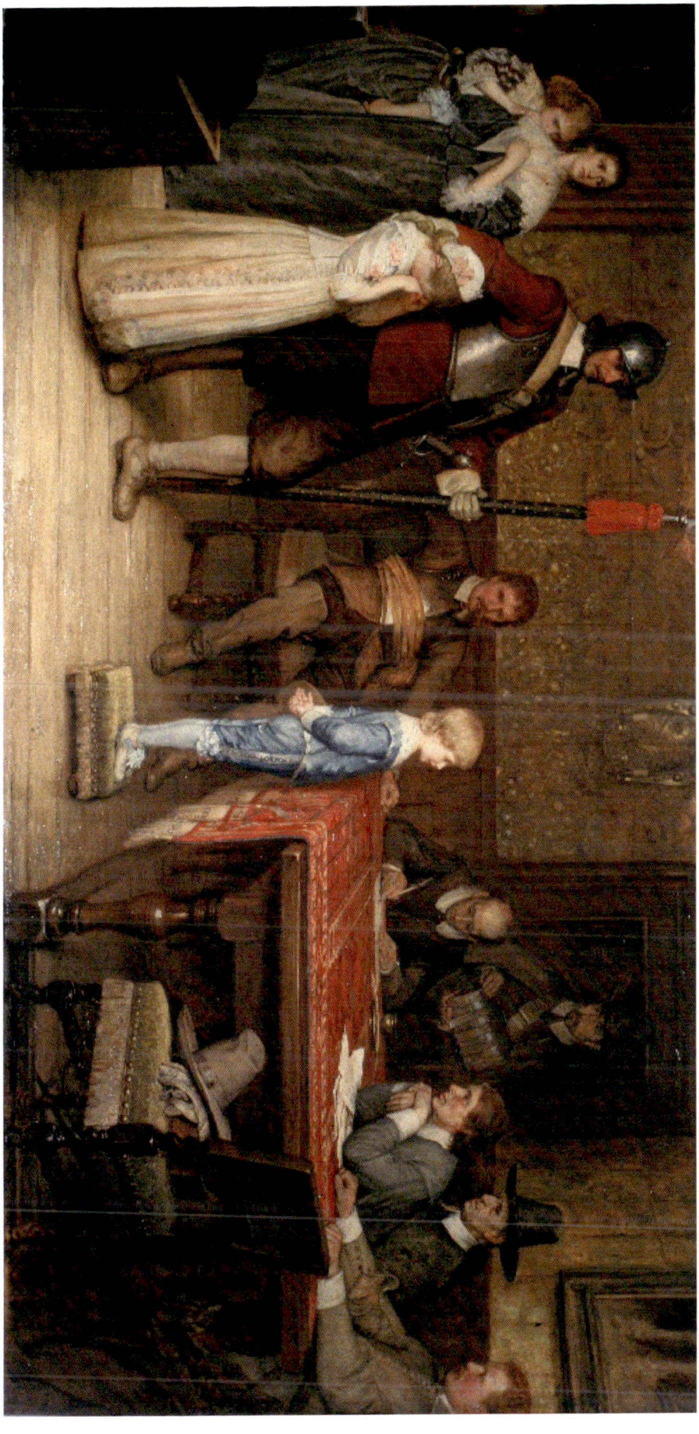

A Street in Brittany, 1881, Stanhope Alexander Forbes (1857-1947)

KNITTING FISHERMEN'S JUMPERS

Skin swollen with water,
his face battered by rocks,
my mother didn't recognise
him, only the sodden jumper
she'd knitted – a tiny green fish
swimming between stripes
under the heavy arm someone
lifted for her to see, before she fell.

My sister knots twine ready
to catch the slippery mass.
Our brothers braving every
weather, storm petrels flying
behind boats like the dark souls
they hold: father riding thermals,
keeping an eye on waves stirring.

I knit sea and sky – a blurry, grey
Cancale dawn as boats come back,
or indigo dusk when they push away.
My fingers slippery from sheep grease,
each stitch tight to keep wind and water
from seeping in, until it's too late.

There are no seams, four needles
hold the weight. I know the pattern
mother taught me by heart. I will
recognise any one of my brothers.
The green fish swimming on
through wool sagged by water,
family knitted into the body,
the bone buttons sewn in pale blue.

Alicia Stubbersfield

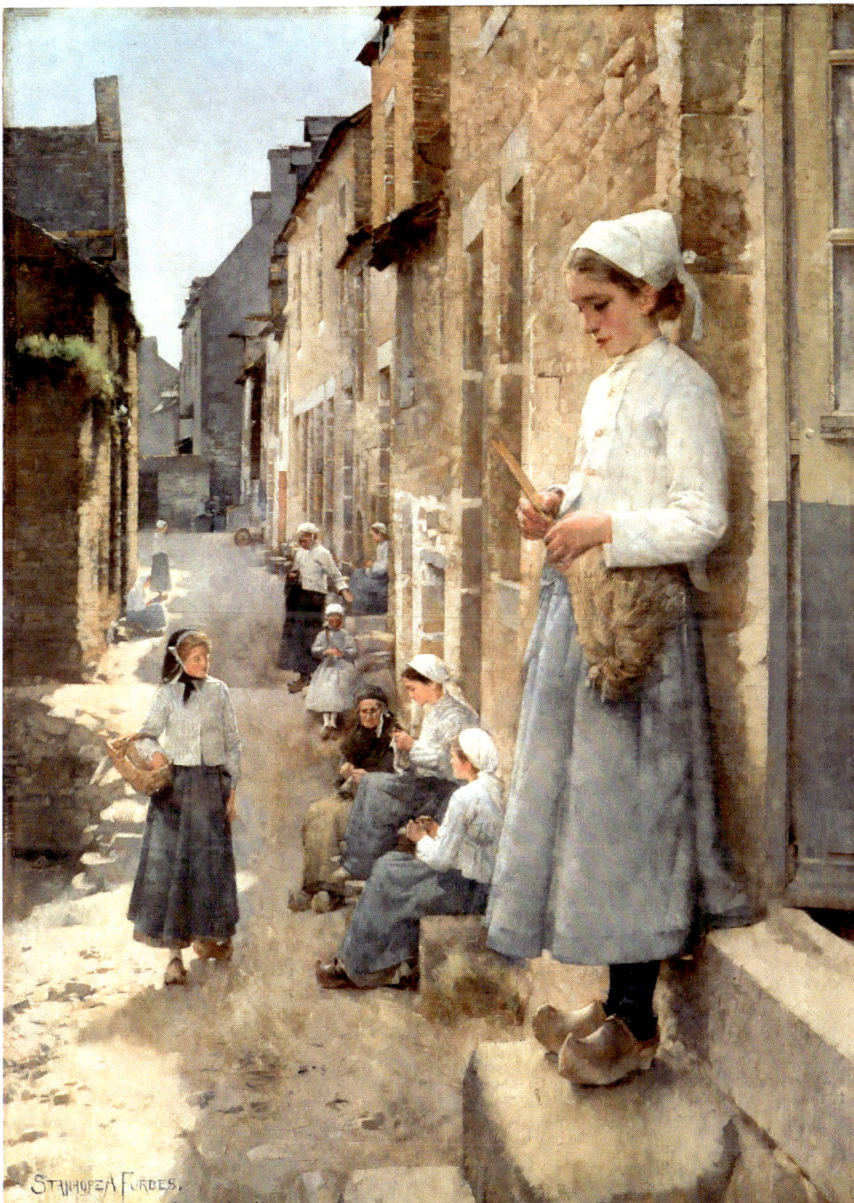
STANHOPE A FORBES.
à Cancale. 1881.

Ville d'Avray, White Houses, 1882, Georges Pierre Seurat (1859-1891)

WHITE HOUSES

Someone else's secrets shuttered here
behind pale walls, the screen of trees.
Security in squares, oblongs –
no hint in this grouping
of nuances of lives, relationships.
Not his concern, otherness
not what he's after, this artist
himself a man of secrets; his stance
from across a cornfield, distance
yielding a safer perspective.

Do these leafy suburbs remind him
how his father withdrew, solitary,
to the fringes of Paris, an allotment?
His seeing brush avoids
engagement with eyes, mouths.
His quest is to dissect the heart
of colour, break open its secret,
dissolve into vibrant seeds, exact
in close coupling.

Of Madeleine Knobloch, his model,
mistress, wife, he gave no hint,
nor of their son Pierre-Georges –
undisclosed to family, friends.
Divisionist technique,
his people part of his pattern, static
as these white houses of Ville d'Avray.

Gladys Mary Coles

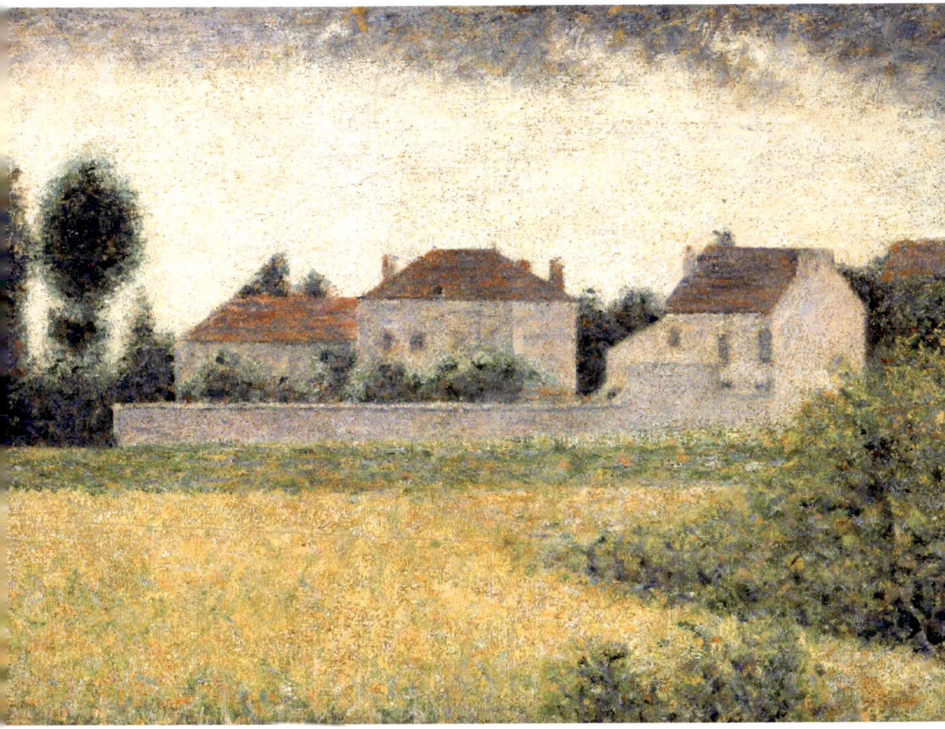

Off to the Fishing Grounds, c. 1885, Stanhope Alexander Forbes (1857-1947)

THERE IS A BOAT DOWN ON THE QUAY

There is a boat down on the quay come home at last.
The paint's chipped, the sails stained as if
Time's pissed up against them.
I imagine the sea-routes it's followed,
Sailing through the world's sunken veins
With its cargo of longings;
A little boat that's nuzzled its way
Into the armpits of forests,
That's sliced through the moon's reflection,
Through the phosphate that clings to the lips of waves.
I knew its crew once,
Those boys manacled to freedom
Who set sail over half a century ago,
And were like giants to me.
A solitary child in awe of oceans
I saw them peel their shadows from the land
And watched them depart.
What did they think when they peered
Over the rim of the world,
Where Time roared and bubbled
And angels swooped like swallows?
Reading an ancient Morse-code of starlight,
Stranded by the longing to be elsewhere,
What secrets did they learn to forget?
I longed to be among them,
A passenger curled up in fate's pocket,
I longed to be a part of them –
Those ghosts who set sail in my childhood,
Those phantoms who shaped me,
That marvelous crew for whom
I have stretched a simple goodbye
Out over a lifetime.

Brian Patten

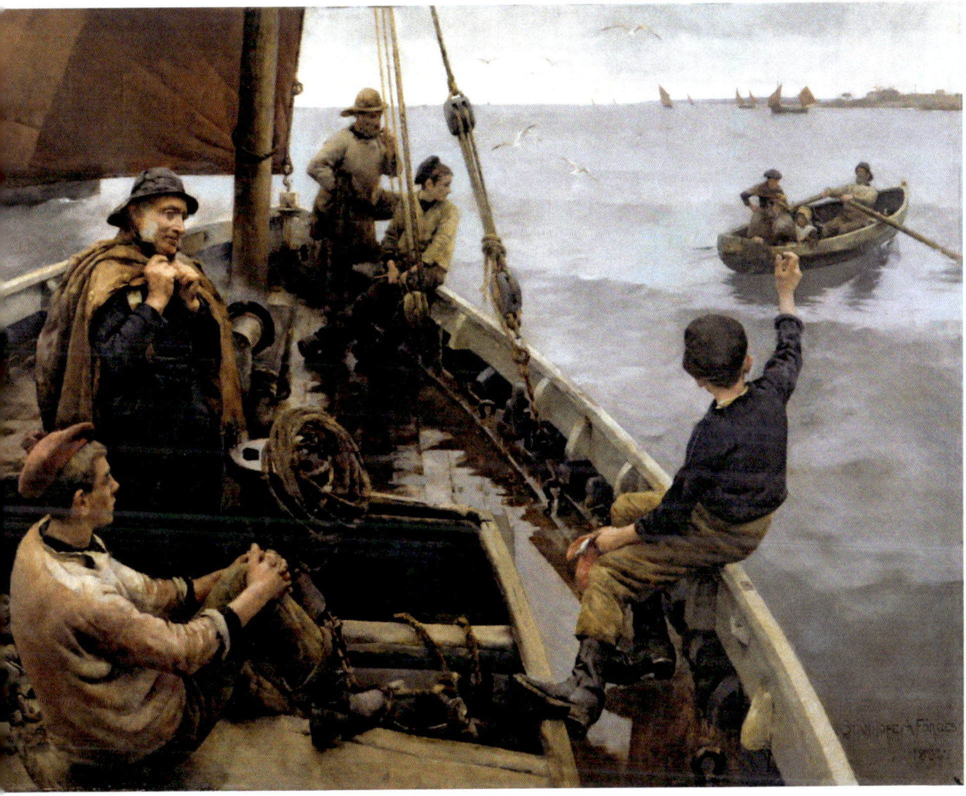

The Promise, 1888, Henry Tuke (1858-1929)

THE PROMISE

1.
The smell of blossom weighs in our nostrils,
sweet as cake on our heavy tongues. I breathe
perfume that stays in me and plants a shadow-tree
stirring in the night wind when I lie alone, branches
lifting against unknown skies. When did I become an orchard?

I'll climb and ride the tree as I've done before.
I tell him, ride the white horse, mane like waves,
ride it when he's gone and think of him, drink in
perfume like the rich, dark rum he'll taste. He flinches,
clutches the tree, says it will be too full of fruit for climbing up

- he means me as he wishes me to be, and I'm not.
Not yet, not yet, my breasts still small, my body light.
I tell him: wait. He sways towards me and away. I'm not afraid.
The tree stands between us, though its perfume knits me to him.
He says he wants me safe. I wonder what he means.

2.
I grasp the tree like the ship's rail, I will not throw
myself over, drown in her dark water,
though I would fall into her, now,
lose myself under this filmy cloud
of perfume and stirring I know
from nights in crow's nests,
vertiginous like this: are they blossoms or stars,
behind me? The sky blooms, I can hardly see her eyes.
The tree interrupts me as the sea will interrupt a man
with its perfume, laughing at promises the wind takes.
She's softness, light, a climber, not a clinging vine.
It's I who cling to the dizzy cloud of tree and her small hand
like dry land, it's I who need anchoring. To leave in spring!
Blossom at flood-tide, perfume billowing that must fill her,
allowing me to follow – to leave now and let her climb, a girl still,
riding the tree of life alone – I would fall into her over the side as sailors do,
as if a plunge in salt would sweeten it, as if they could plumb her long deeps.

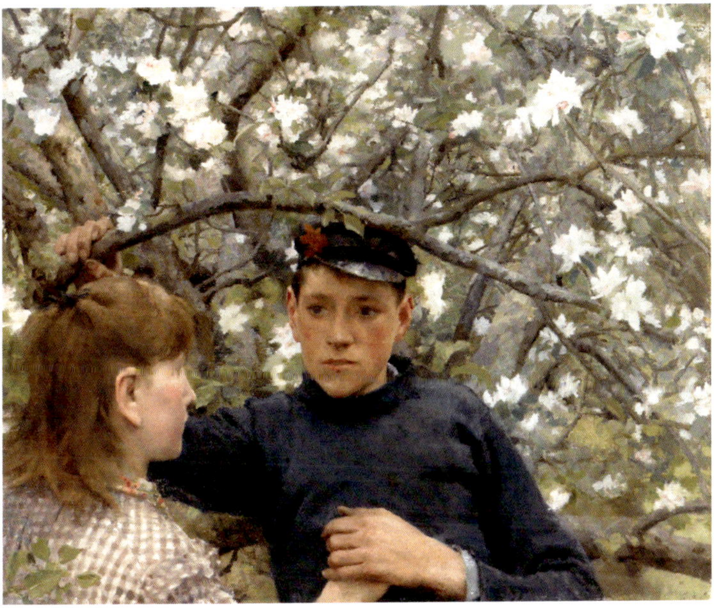

3.
Don't, please. I'll be blamed again. Tree of life, indeed! The stories they spin
to convince themselves of their uprightness! The garden, the tree. Always
the tree. The snake incidental, a branch swaying in the wind, offering,
in the language all human beings speak, what all human beings crave
- and turn from. When we grow needles, embroider with the sun's gold threads,
native Americans call us the Grandmothers, weavers who can't be bent
to the death-trade. Most of us are fair game for strange fruit, crucified,
lynched, hanged by dint of so-called law. Some clinch their own fates,
the Judas deed. We weep for it, they say. It may be. There are no willows
in the cherry orchard made into a symbol by the coughing Russian with his
blossoms of blood and word. Eden reborn, re-mourned. The past flows in my bark,
a river streaming to the tallest tip by centrifugal force, changing course in autumn
- when these two will be far apart, he drawing into port, she watching me,
my river flowing down through tributary roots. I see her sweeping leaves into a bonfire
the opposite of Dido's on her lonely shore, as bees that circle me now, die
and perfumed women reach their white arms towards him – I tell you something,
even a man about to dance from the end of a rope will flinch from a bee.

Aileen La Tourette

The Funeral of Shelley, 1889, Louis Edouard Fournier (*1857-1917*)

BRIGHT SHADOW (8 July, 1822)

Smoke greys his hair, counterfeiting
age, years he'll never live,
years which might have modified
his radical spirit. Now he's a Guy Fawkes
feeding the flames, his pyre a bed of branches,
roots of ancient pine, perfumed by frankincense,
infused with libations of oil and wine –
and layered with lime.

He was the merman who couldn't swim,
a sailor who couldn't navigate,
forever flirting with water, the element
not his own – a firefly who drowned.

Too much sail on his lovely, lethal schooner
manned by his friend Williams and a boatboy,
he left Livorno, immersed in Keats' *Lamia*.
Never to reach Lerici, lost in a storm cloud,
plunged thirteen fathoms down.

There's fiction in Fournier's funeral scene –
his artistic lie tunes the mood, subdues
the blazing blue of sky and sea.
Here's a likeness of Shelley, though his face and flesh
were gone, devoured in the deep.
The chief mourners are classically grouped:
pensive, haunted and beautiful, Byron looks
for an escape – at any moment now
he'll run naked into the sea;
next to Byron, Leigh Hunt stands sorrowing
yet he remained inside his carriage throughout the ritual;
and Mary Shelley, shown kneeling on the beach, was elsewhere –
barred by her gender, weeping in the Casa Magni.

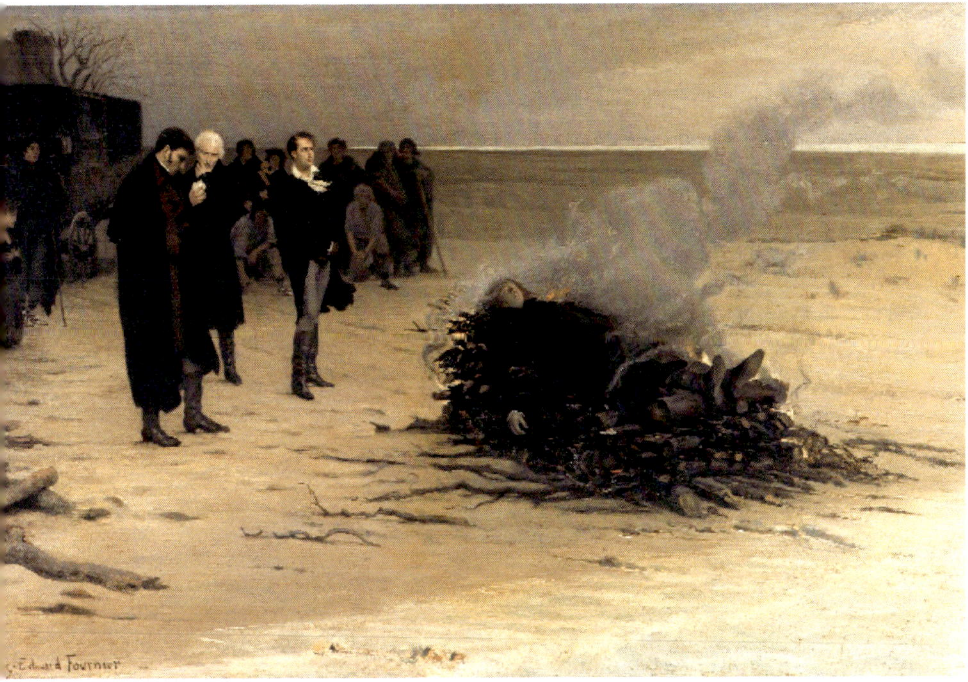

Trelawny's deep in grief and concentration –
as the flames bite, he'll orate his pagan farewell
to his friend, this atheist who sought the Devil, in love
with abstracts and absolutes – Beauty, Liberty, Joy.
I restore to nature through fire the elements
of which this man was composed, earth, air and water.
Everything is changed but not annihilated. He is now
a portion of that which he worshipped.
And when the body falls apart, Trelawny
will scorch his hands snatching out
the heart.

Gladys Mary Coles

Break-up of the ice on the Seine, c.1890, Claude Monet (1840-1926)

RIVER

River, I come with no rudder
to shatter your ice – no long oars
to scratch shallows
where water-lice suckle
on the flash of metallic spoke and all that

rubber. River, your head's choked
with a city's forgotten journeys: car-rides
to parties, seasides, offices,
morgues and your mind

is stone-weighted skirts and sacks
heavy with infant dogs – the dead strips of bark
that have fallen to roughen
your fugues.

The sleepless have fed you
their thick foamy pads, stained
with the syrups of birth, death
and the crazed killings
of time inbetween

your banks: the hardcrocks
of frozen mudbone
where sprites loiter
and whisper fishy parables
to reeds.

River, you cannot go on
like this.

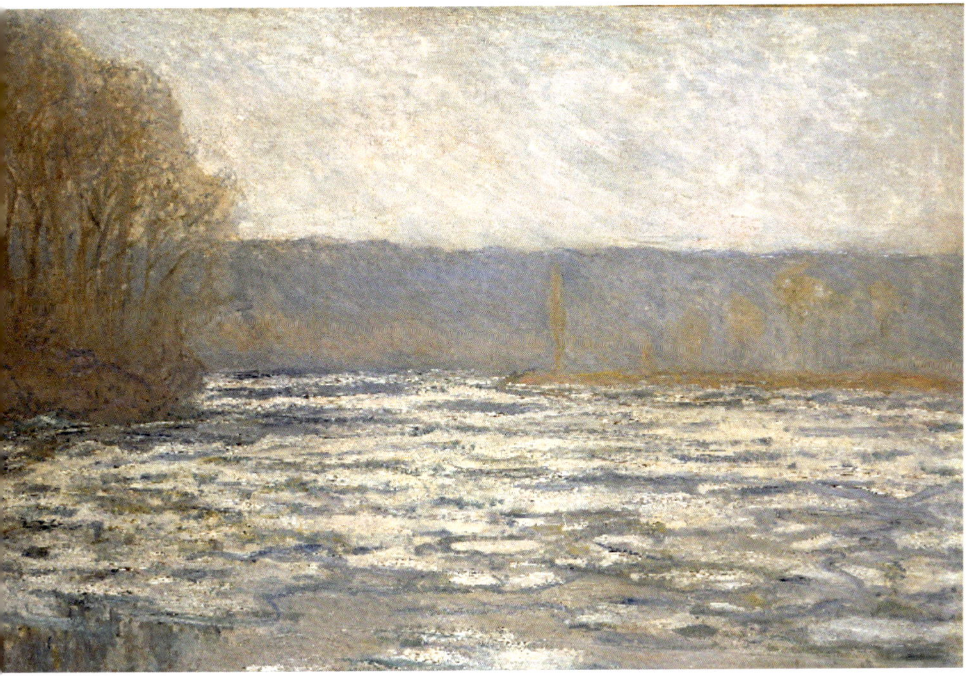

Bring back the ducks and the quacks
in long coats and latex boots – sleek
rods rousing the larvae
that have slept in your stamens
all winter.

Bring back the soft deck of long grass,
leaf, flower and moss. Let river
boats tug away
your hypothermic
coma.

Janette Stowell

The Sense of Sight, 1895, Annie Louisa Swynnerton (1844-1933)

PARADISE 33

A 'version' of Dante Alighieri

Thus my sight, becoming purified, entered
further into the radiance of the clear light
which itself is the nature of truth

and henceforth all that I saw surpassed our speech.

Like one who has seen a vision in a dream
and, after dreaming, finds only
an imprinted passion remains:

such am I. Though my vision be all but ceased
the sweetness born of it
perfects itself still in my heart.

Like this the snow is opened in the sun
and the sayings of the sibyl lost
on the wind in the rising leaves.

Ade Jackson

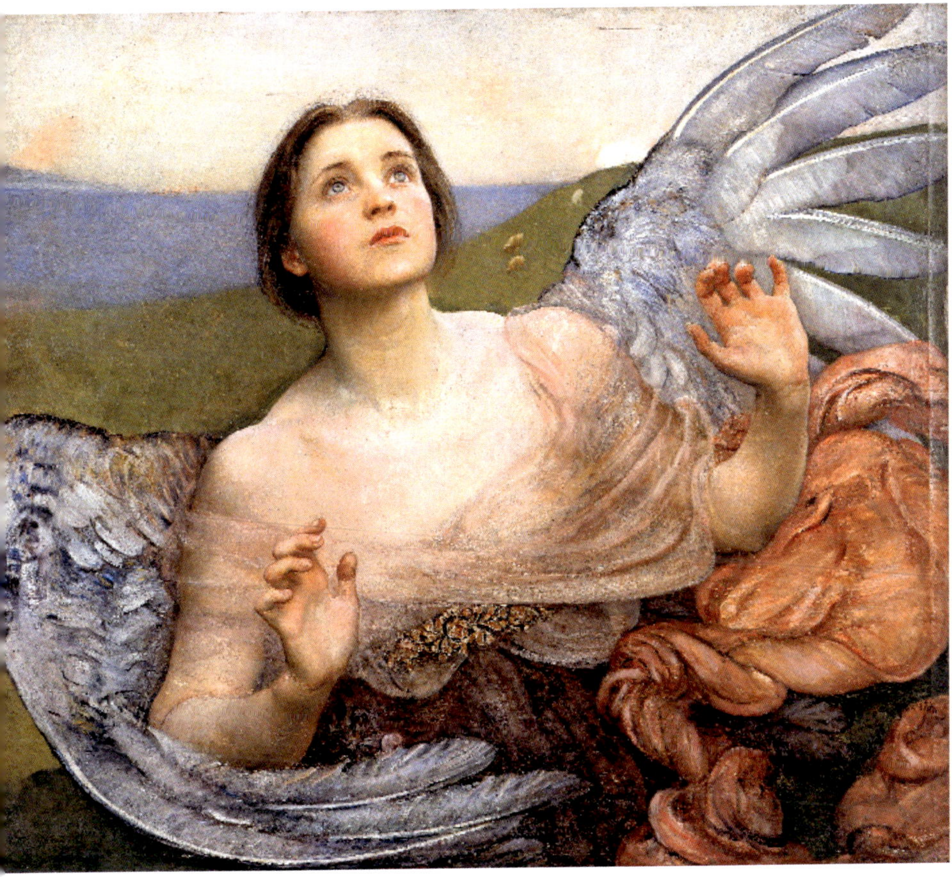

Strangers in a Strange Land, 1898, Albert Starling (1878-1922)

I DANCE BUT ONLY WITH MY FEET

Here on the quayside
dancing on my make-shift stage,
I notice many things, and people.
Like how naturally, casually
the fishermen treat their catch.

The lovely gold-flecked
thick-fleshed plaice,
the gleaming silver herring.

I wish the fish could be our reward,
it would be worth much more than coin.
Although now I see the money
flash and glint in the old man's hat –
oh I *wish* that my father could learn how to fish
then maybe I need not have to dance at all.

The men meet here every day.
The old one with sad eyes
never watches me but looks beyond.
Maybe he's seen too many dancing children.

I remember our journey,
our herded, huddled voyage.
Father, Mother, their arguments
to leave or not to leave
the hiss-whispering threats behind.
It made me afraid.

But now, although the north-east wind
bites through our thin clothes just as it did then
and I dance only with my feet
I feel the sun shines brighter here
because people seem unafraid.

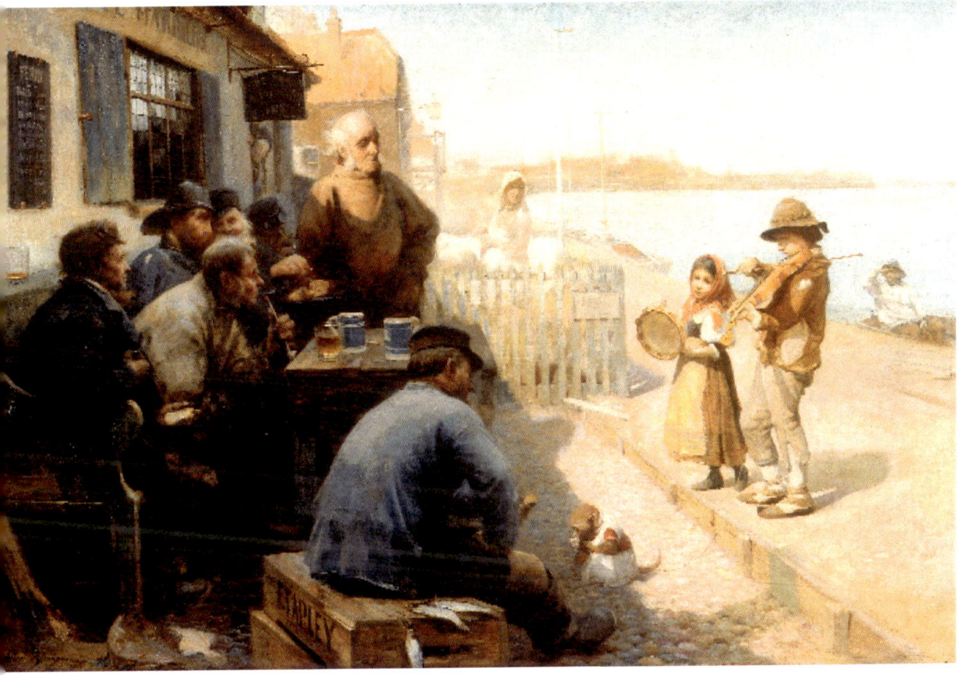

So perhaps one day
when Mother has enough fish to pickle and salt
and we can have chicken soup and chalahs every day,
and she can bake the lovely chanuka
all heavy with fruit and spice –
perhaps we too will be happy and unafraid.

Jacquiline Baker

Madame Hessel on the Sofa, c.1900, Edouard Vuillard (1868-1940)

MADAME HESSEL ON THE SOFA

I've painted you in tea gowns and kimonos. Tea gowns, we both know,
clothe the *four-to-five*, the hour of adultery, in gossamer, easy of access –
- you wore yours for me, pale, peach-coloured silk blossoming over your body like a sai
of chastity – your husband Jos pays for paint I pour as you pour tea –

pouring from my brush, a million masks for your unknown, familiar face.
Can he not tell my knowledge is Venetian, from the Mardi Gras mask that shadows you?
Only a lover knows so little and so much. Can Jos not trace my love-strokes
in the movements of my brush? Can he not see how you lean back in the gondola

I push with my brush down the Grand Canal of art, disguise and love?
Can he not see you laugh behind the mask? Your eyes squinch to slits,
give nothing away. Your lips curve above your adorable chin, the seat of your will
- fierce as the heat we make. His paintings hang behind you like a dowry.

Your chemise is white, not bridal, meant for a laughing matron cosseted on all sides
by cushions plump as buttocks. We've plumped those cushions, flattened them with
our own. Your face trusts my silence. My hands can span your waist, at which
I place the shadow of a purse. Your lips will tighten their own strings at this.

Your hips glide towards me on the daybed, you spread under your clothes, mermaid
on a rock, fish-skirt finned around your feet – if you have feet – more glistening seal
than mermaid or matron, you eye me, sleek, playful, untouchable, listening to all
I cannot say. The painted water laps at canvas and upholstery, twin fabrics of our fate.

Aileen La Tourette

Vuillard was a good friend of the Hessels. Jos Hessel was his art dealer, whose wife, Lucie, is the subject of the painting.

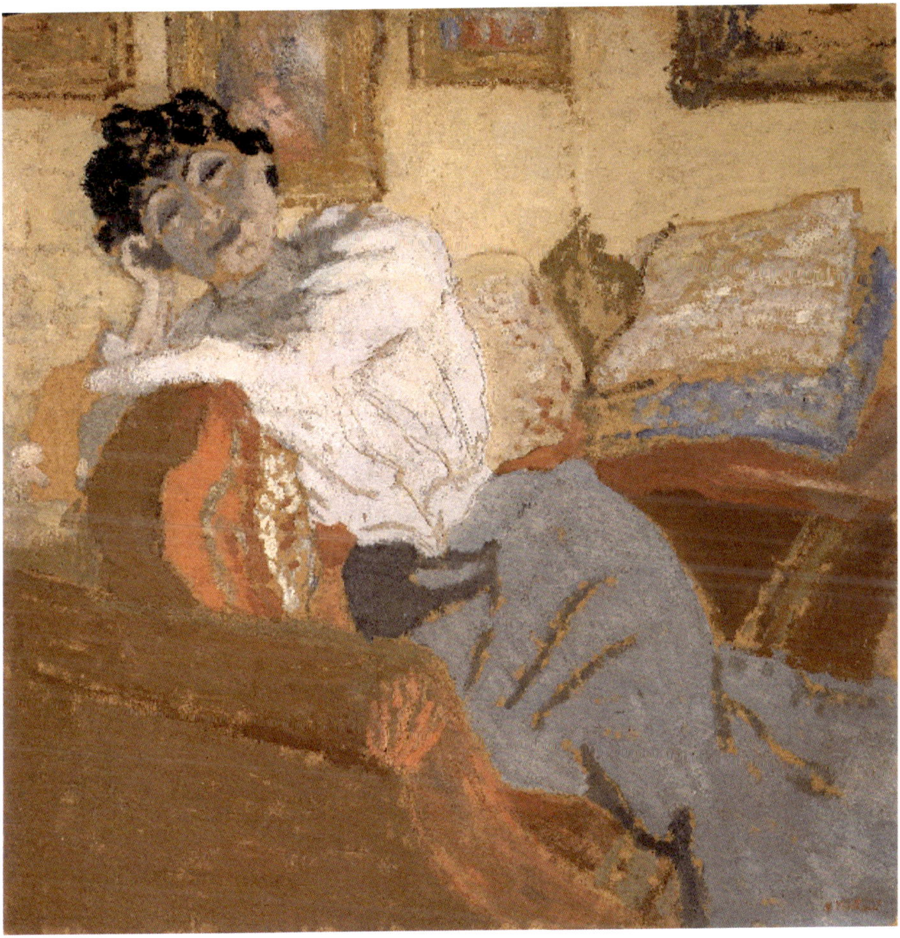

Portrait of Pau Cucurny with a dog, 1903, Pablo Picasso (1881-1973)

STRONG GAZING

The eyes of that Andalucian are killing me

- Luis de Góngora

Pablo Diego José Francisco de Paula Juan Nepomuceno María de los Remedios Crispín Crispiniano Santísima Trinidad Ruiz y Picasso:

I am Picasso, torero,
proud of my burly line
as I lunge, step back and eyeball
the rich man's son, Cucurny,
in my suit of magenta lights.
My line leaps down his shoulders,
captures his sideways list,
cuts his arm off at the wrist.
I give him small holes for eyes,
a weak man's moustache,
zigzag the shadow gathering at his back.

Feo (the tavern dog):

That's me in the right-hand corner,
my smudged brown chops held high
at a rumour of tripe from a passing waiter's tray.
Can you tell from my collar
that I belong to the tavern
and not to this out-of-place client
buttoned into his Chesterfield coat?
Now that the tripe has passed
I haruspicate his drawers,
a quivering nosegay of bachelor starch and shit,
of a bull spewing seed into the artist's hands.

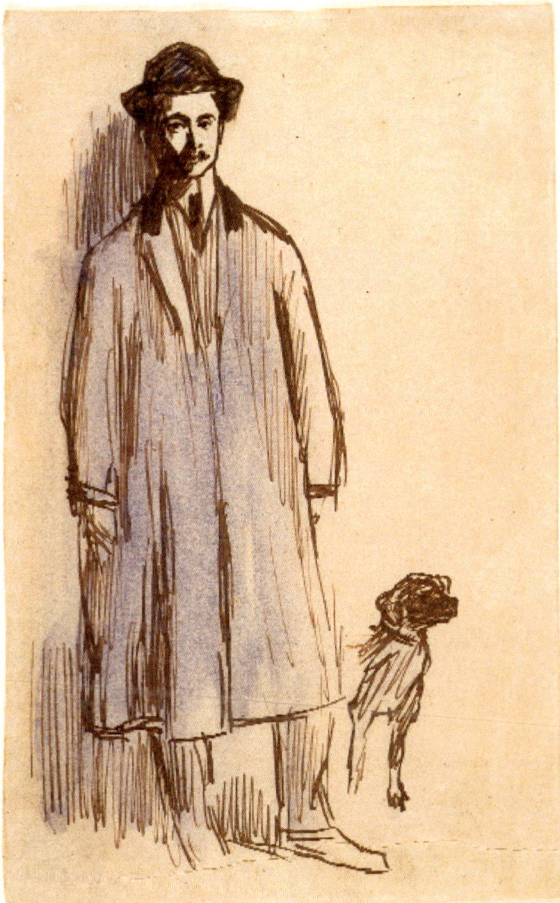

Pau Cucurny (the subject):

Picasso slunk home from Paris
skint, his tail between his legs
but here at Els Quatre Gats
he squanders my money on cronies
who stamp their feet and applaud him
as they guzzle Domecq and smoked cod.
His artist's eyes are fingers, probing, holding.
He hands me the sketch. I see
a cartoon of a bullock
dressed in a hat and coat,
a stab of black tie at its throat.

Jenny Newman

Blackberry Gathering, 1912, Elizabeth Adela Forbes (1859-1912)

BLACKBERRY GATHERING

How hidden the hard labour of this blouse,
its gleam, my flag of white high on this hill.
Our feet have burned to reach these treasures, fill
this pewter pail, light basket, bowl; I pause,
the sun burns where he gathered up my hair
(our daughters' heads protected from its touch)
the spark of him inside me like a watch
as scents and seeds of summer fill the air.
Embroidery of fruit pricks both my hands,
dreams red upon my skin like work, like fire.
The child within me kicks; I'll pray each boot
from him. We gather in, as God commands.
Home, sweet feast, the cool cream from our larder.
And how I'll stuff my husband's mouth with fruit.

Pauline Rowe

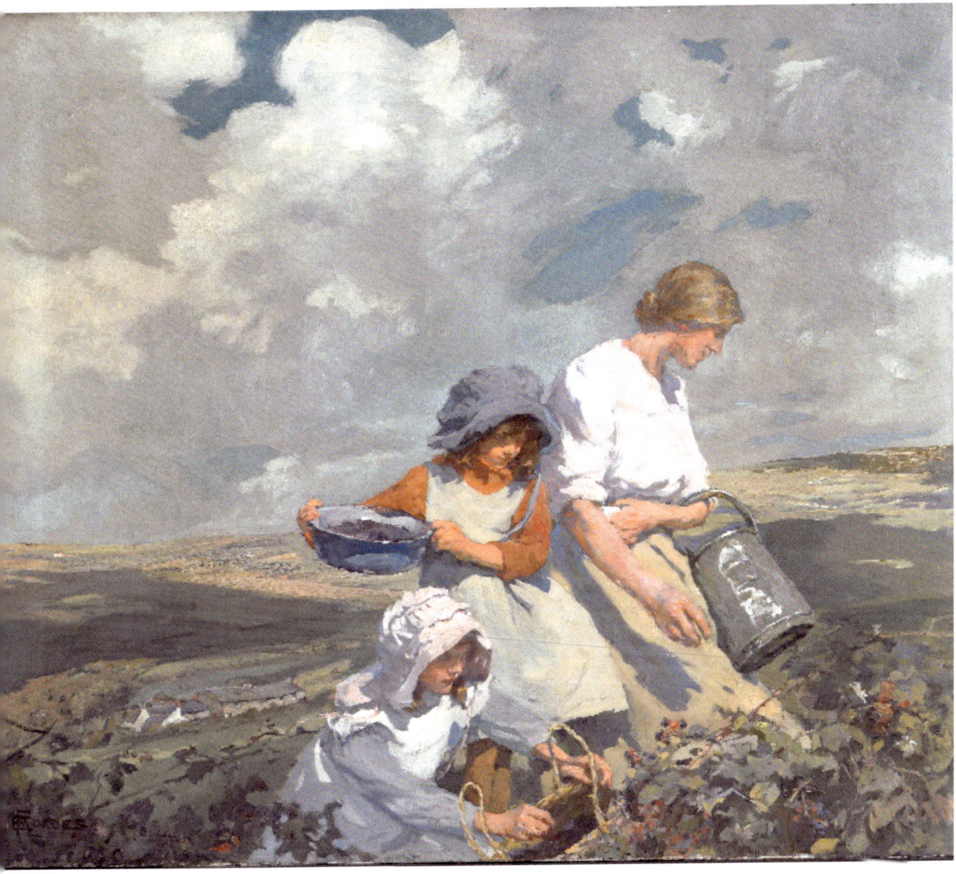

Fancy Dress, Miss Beerbohm, 1916, Walter Sickert (1860-1942)

THE GREEN DRESS

I borrowed this dress off my sister
He told me to get up posh
Well I don't have anything fancy
So I took her best satin frock

Look how it shines in the sun's rays
The fabric so smooth – its sheen
Catching those shafts through the curtains –
Such a glorious shade of green

I met him down the Old Bedford
He's often there watching the shows
Sal says he's keen on us dancers
Always sits in the plushest front row

He made sure I could make it for Wednesday
He even came round to the house
To escort me – I felt like a duchess
Well these days you hardly go out
There's a killer loose on the streets with a knife
Cuts the throats of women out at night
Emily Dimmock got murdered nearby
Round the corner opposite

He asks will I stay here till after dark
He'll pay me a few extra shillings
Cooped up here, I'll be safer than safe
He just wants to paint my skin

Dymphna Callery

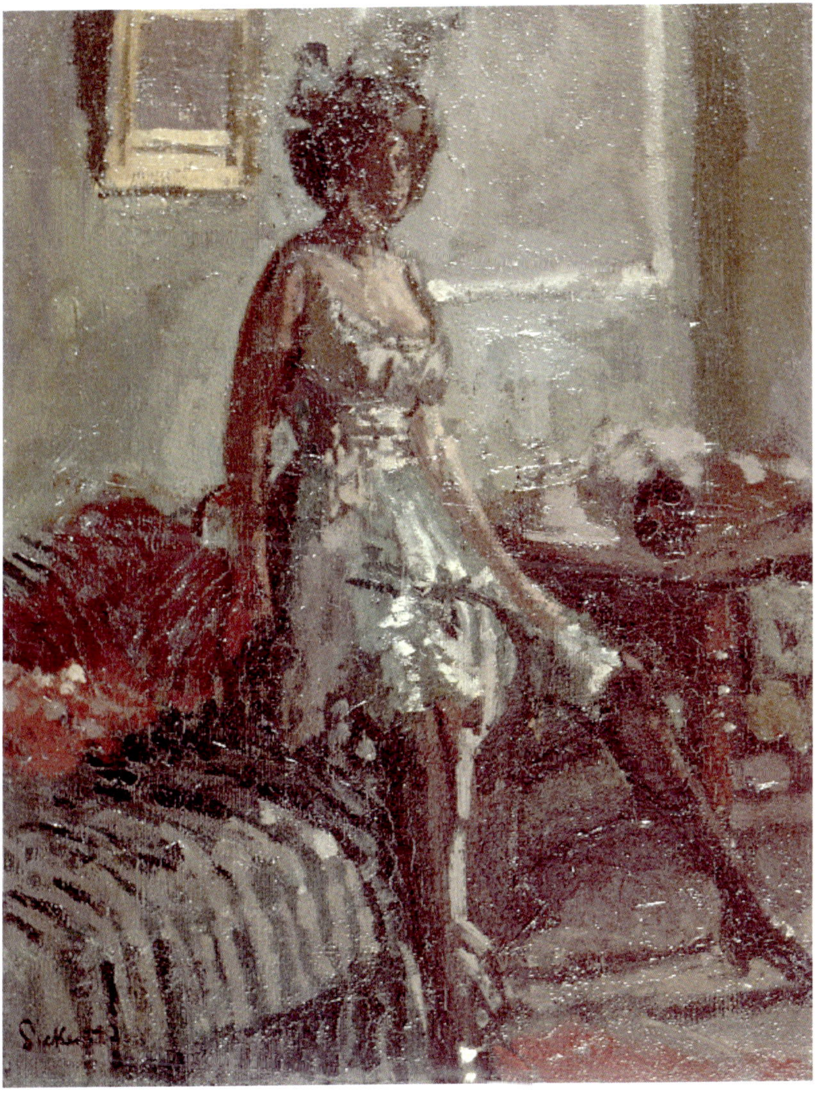

An Old Inn Kitchen, 1922, Frederick William Elwell (1870-1958)

OLD INN KITCHEN

He says us girls'll be the death of him
But that's not true. I seen the way he looks at us.
He's like my Dad was once, before
He went away to war and lost his wits
And Ma left home and all of us split up
And lucky me the only one of all of us
To get a berth like this. Me only twelve
When he took me on, that scared I was
Homesick for Ma and all. He might of took
Advantage. There's many does.
He never.

They keep me young,
These Yorkshire lassies. Feather-headed,
Flighty, forgetful, the lot of them. But then:
They keep me on my toes. If Effie hadn't died
My own girls might have been their age.
I worry like a father. This place – I'm settled
Here, I like it. But there's dangers for a lass.
It's up to me to see they don't get into trouble,
To keep them safe. And train them up.
They'd get a place in service any day
With what I've taught them.

What happened to them once,
What might have happened since –
This moment on a sunny afternoon
Is all we have.
And all we have
Is now – our past like theirs
Past, our future as unreal.
Only
This moment, these friends, this sunshine,
This happiness. Now.

R.V. Bailey

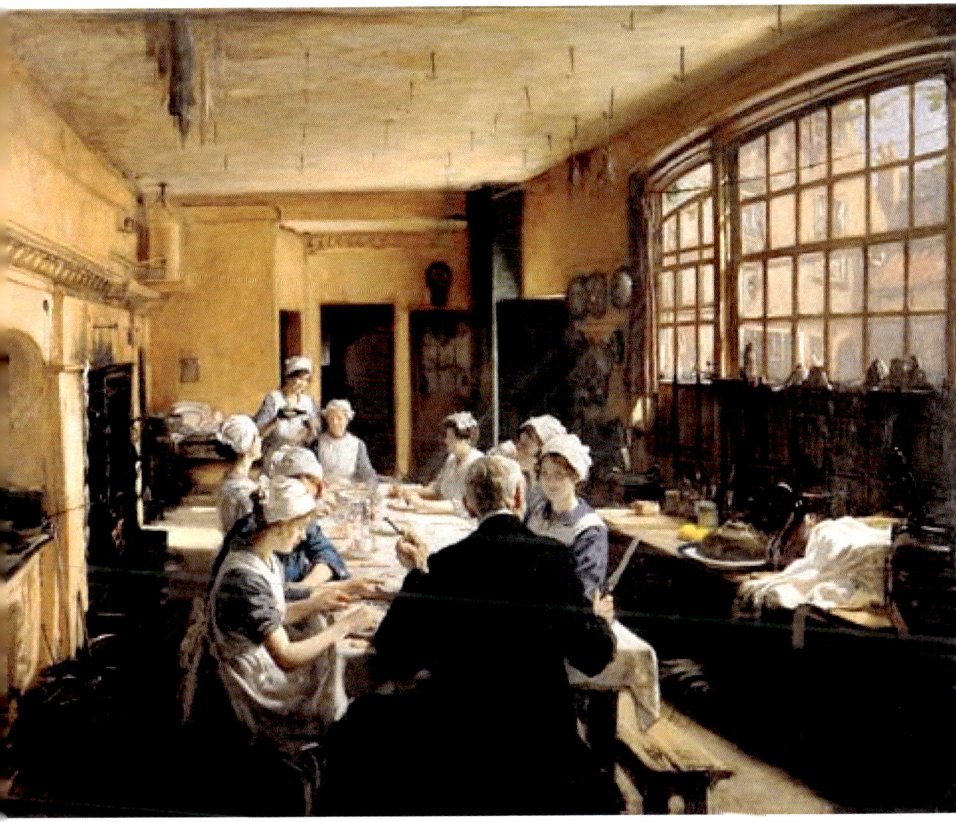

Israfel, 1930, Jacob Epstein (1880-1959)

ISRAFEL

You're wondering where my wings are. Your fingers itch to lift my bronze
hair, check for scars or stumps. *Wings aren't hacked off for nothing*,
you're thinking, story-hungry, zipping through your Angel file,
- Lucifer, the Fall, something juicier - Israfel, *The Burning One*.
Hellfire. Hot pants without seams. Black wings fanning us like twin beech trees,
sequinned with stars – I'd do you in a human heartbeat, carbon prodigy,

only where I'm coming from, you're way underage. I rocked your
cradle – Islamic angel given form here by a Jew – (sweet Christianity
would give me sugared feathers, a bath in bleach). The Koran says
my heart-strings are a lute, I have the sweetest voice of all God's creatures –
that word. *Sweet*. Know what it means? Not grains you sprinkle into
tannin and caffeine. More like wine in your bloodstream. Venom and truth serum.

Dark Edgar had me, poor cloaked Edgar, ravening in sweeping black with a croak
from the heart – *None sing so wildly well/ as the angel Israfel*
- even Edgar chose the lute. What I raise to my lips is scorching, blowtorch
brass. But a bust can't blow a trumpet, even dangle it
from fingers nicotined gold, swing the lighted tip.
He wanted me demobbed: no feathers, no bling,

the better to catch me at my day job. Listening.
Don't bother squinting at my empty sockets, looking
for your picture. They echo like Sibyl's cave
with your riddles. I overhear you for a living, chatterbox,
God's eavesdropper, got it? Angel Radio, tuned to your frequencies
with no off switch. Right now you're thinking *so there is a God*.

Look at the hair, alive as Medusa's – your sound waves stone me,
curl my aerials like hot rollers, twist every filament
with your humidities, ripple me like sand, on top. You're my hairdresser,
your parties buff my coiffure like conditioner, your downers steam
the mirror, frizz this mop to kingdom come. Your blues get bluer
every year, I swear to what is not. But heaven listens. Edgar got that.

Stars flock to your spotlit rooms, read your lips through
glass curtains. You're their stars, I guess. Not that the sun
goes round you, don't get big boots again. You're my soundtrack.
Can't block my ears. What with? Busts suck. Can't jam
a syllable, squeeze off a wavelength. I read you, baby.
Alpha. Bravo. Charlie. Delta. Echo. Foxtrot... Omega. (Just in case).

Aileen La Tourette

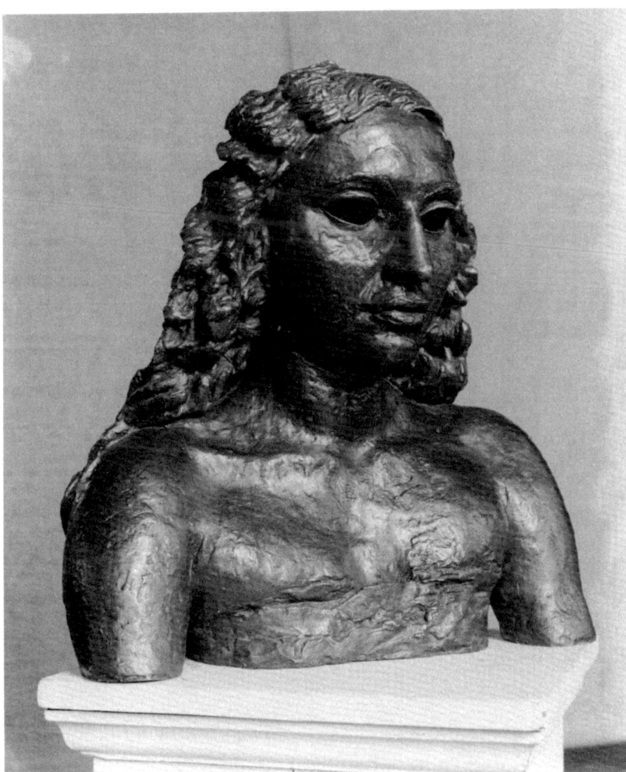

Springtime in Eskdale, 1935, James McIntosh Patrick (1907-1998)

SPRING MORNING

Light lies in lemons and limes,
slices the lines of trees,
limns mossy trunks and greenish stone,
skims surfaces and brushes in another day.

Sleeping cat shadows lie on the hill
as cloud encroaches on the sunwashed dale,
melting the citrus lemons and limes
to the watered hues of a northern spring.

New leaves jiggle somewhere
between blue and yellow, stippling
sunskydistance, forming
shaded depths in secret spaces.

A boy starts down a crooked path,
dreaming of structures, building
bridges between land and light,
and the words in my head flutter
a pathway between in and out,
where I may play with tone and view
how paint and paper labels parody the fire,
the way lemons and limes lie in the light.

Carol Fenlon

The painting depicts 'The Crooks' in Eskdalemuir, Dumfriesshire, Scotland, birthplace of the engineer Thomas Telford (1757-1834).

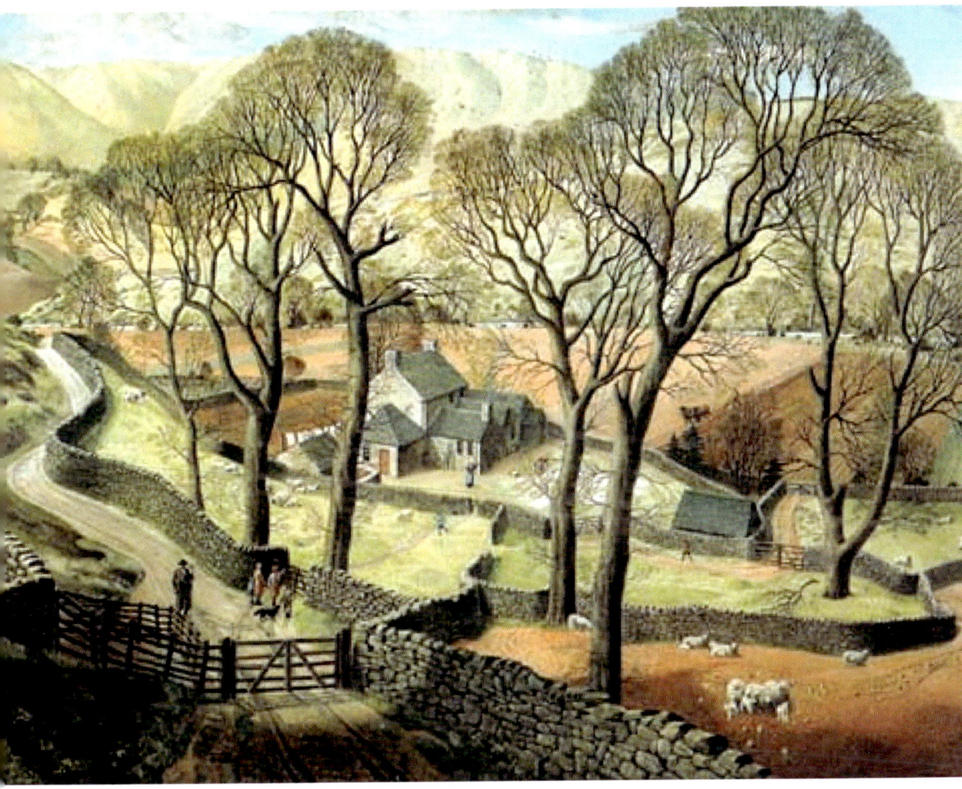

The Fever Van, 1935, Lawrence Stephen Lowry (1887-1976)

THE FEVER VAN

Everyone is staring; the doors are open,
The one with fever is pushed inside.
And three dogs stand or walk down the street.

I dreamed about those dogs last night;
Their eyes like the inside of a greasy hat,
Their tongues the shifting shape of smoke.

We are the spirit of the Fever Van they said,
We are the spirit of the Fever Van
And then, because it was a dream and I was frightened,

All those people who were staring climbed in
And the Fever Van was my head, hollow and waiting for fever
Like that three-dog, smoke-shaped, dark-sky

Moment before a poem or a painting is born.

Ian McMillan

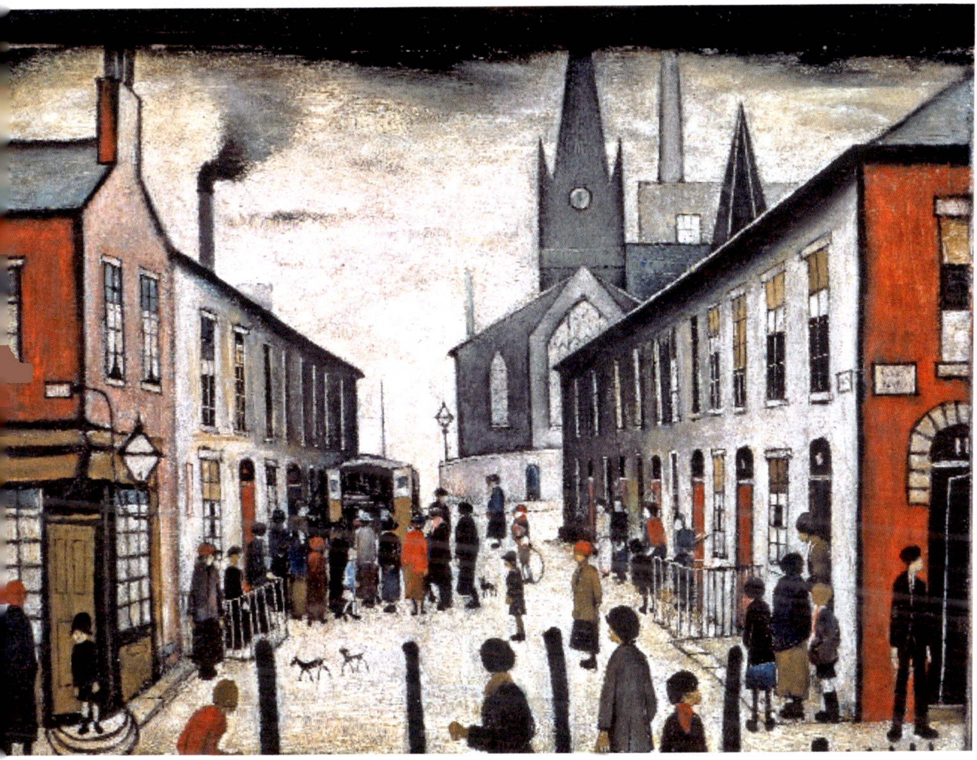

The Student, 1938, Thomas Burke (1906-45)

THE STUDENT

Milton, Donne, Dryden and Dante,
All heroes, my inspiration and fuel for my aspirations.
I read, I learn and admire these literary lions
As daily I study the masters' syntax,
Their style, their artistry.
My hope – to emulate their greatness
And become a master story-teller.

Words, sentences, similes and syllables
Dance a tarantella around my troubled mind.
How can the brain give full due
To poetry, plays and literary love,
When the rent must be paid
And my aching fragile frame yearns
For tender mutton or a hearty Irish stew.

For months I toil and strive for perfection,
Long nights scribbling and starving by candlelight,
But finally my manuscript masterpiece is complete.
I submit my first novel and wait, and patiently wait.
At last a publisher's note, I tremble
As I fumble to open – a rejection letter.
Alas, only literary succour again for supper.

Lynn Pegler

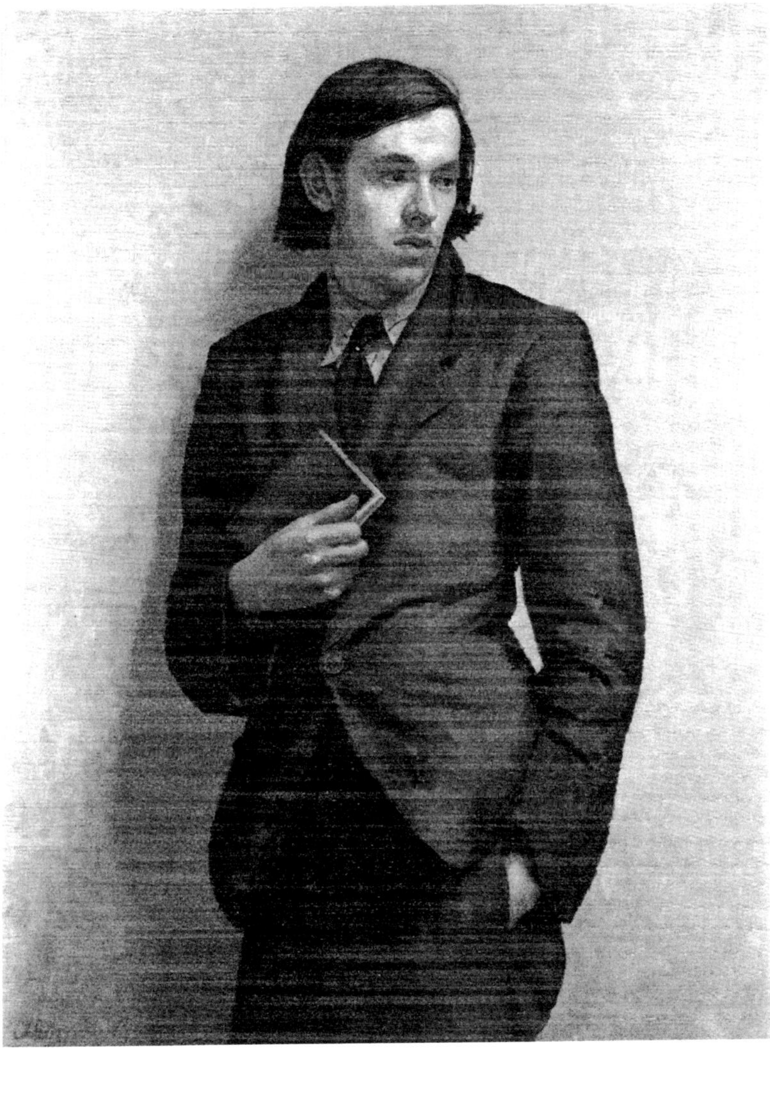

Baby in pram in garden, 1956, John Bratby (1928-92)

PAINT

He dreams in colour.

Red is lust, hair, rage.
Pale pink, a lover's cheeks; coral, her kiss.
A flaring match: chrysanthemums and rust.
Blue – rivered veins, tired eyes, the steady hiss of gas fires.
Charcoal's darning wool, work shirts;
while broken slates shine silver, stained by rain.
White's clouds, stiff cotton sheets, a milky breast,
a seagull, paper.
Black, a creaking pram.

Light pewters broken windows; peeling wood
rots mustard with a Tomcat's bitter spray.

An ochre wetness clots his boots like blood:
the cadmium of brickness, crimson clay
a curving, gritty womb to hold a child.
Soft almond blankets rucked under his chin,
a linen pillow cradling his head –

The unexpected pain of loving him...

The painter sleeps, slumped low. His fingers skim
a mug scummed brown with tea. Outside someone
is banging on the door, but still he dreams
of orange houses, olive grass,
his son.

Sarah Maclennan

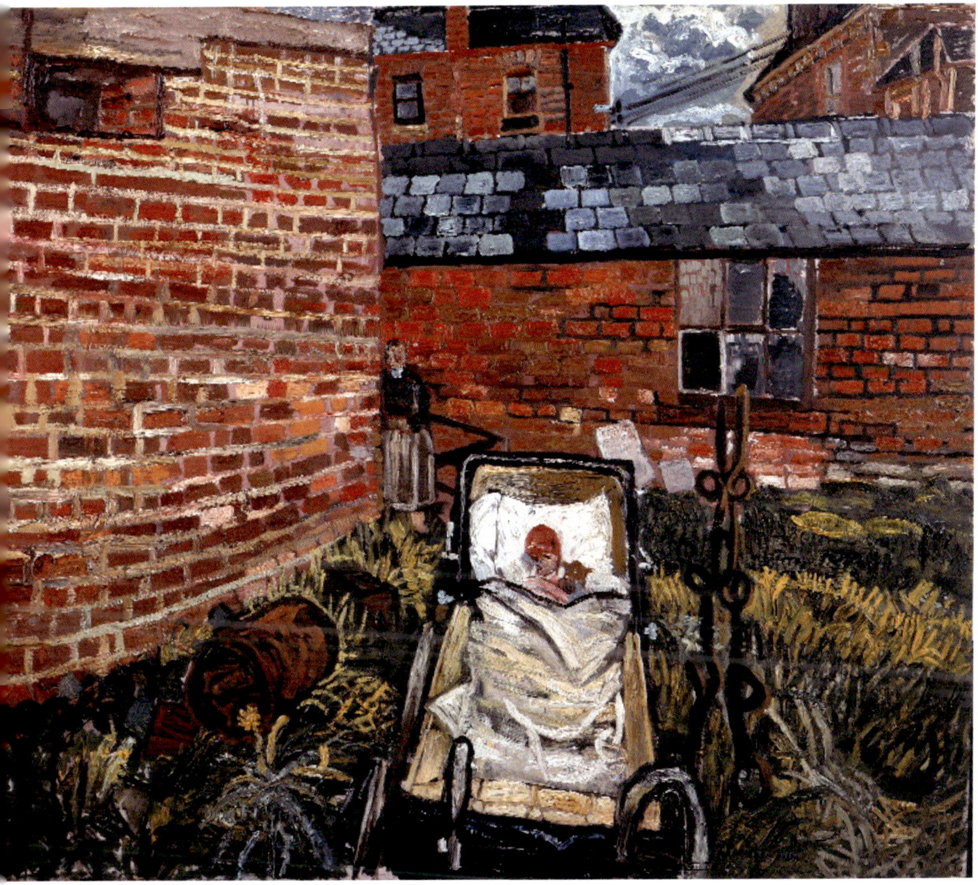

Three Self-portraits with a White Wall, 1957, John Bratby (1928-92)

ENIGMA

He paints as though he had only one more day to live – John Berger

Did narcissism, need or homage to tradition
inspire this enigmatic triple self?
The artist self-caught at different times;
first in the act, brush unseen in outstretched hand,
then standing in smoke-wreathed contemplation
of his choice of triptych for this painting
which with the crosses behind him on the wall
hint at an awareness of vocation;
and finally, job done, about to leave the frame.
Say what you like, it makes you stop and stare
struck by the size, the boldly laid-on paint
the no-nonsense postures, sure handling of the form:
Bratby's craft showing craft at work.

Fame called on Bratby early: prizes, praise, commissions,
that film his paintings set ablaze: then came the Pop Art coup
and the carping from some critics who
had hailed him as the angry future
king of kitchen sinkery
next in line for coronation.

The labelling changed: word was he'd lost his way, broken down,
become banal, too interested in profit; and, worse, was painting
dull portraits of his family, friends, celebrities, himself.

But here's a thought: on a wall elsewhere in Liverpool
you might come upon a challenging late Bratby
(three years before he died) old, half blind and toothless,
the self-depiction honest, unselfpitying, ruthless.

Genius or journeyman? See for yourself and choose.
And, for what it's worth I'd write him down
as the one who kept the contract with his muse.

David Evans

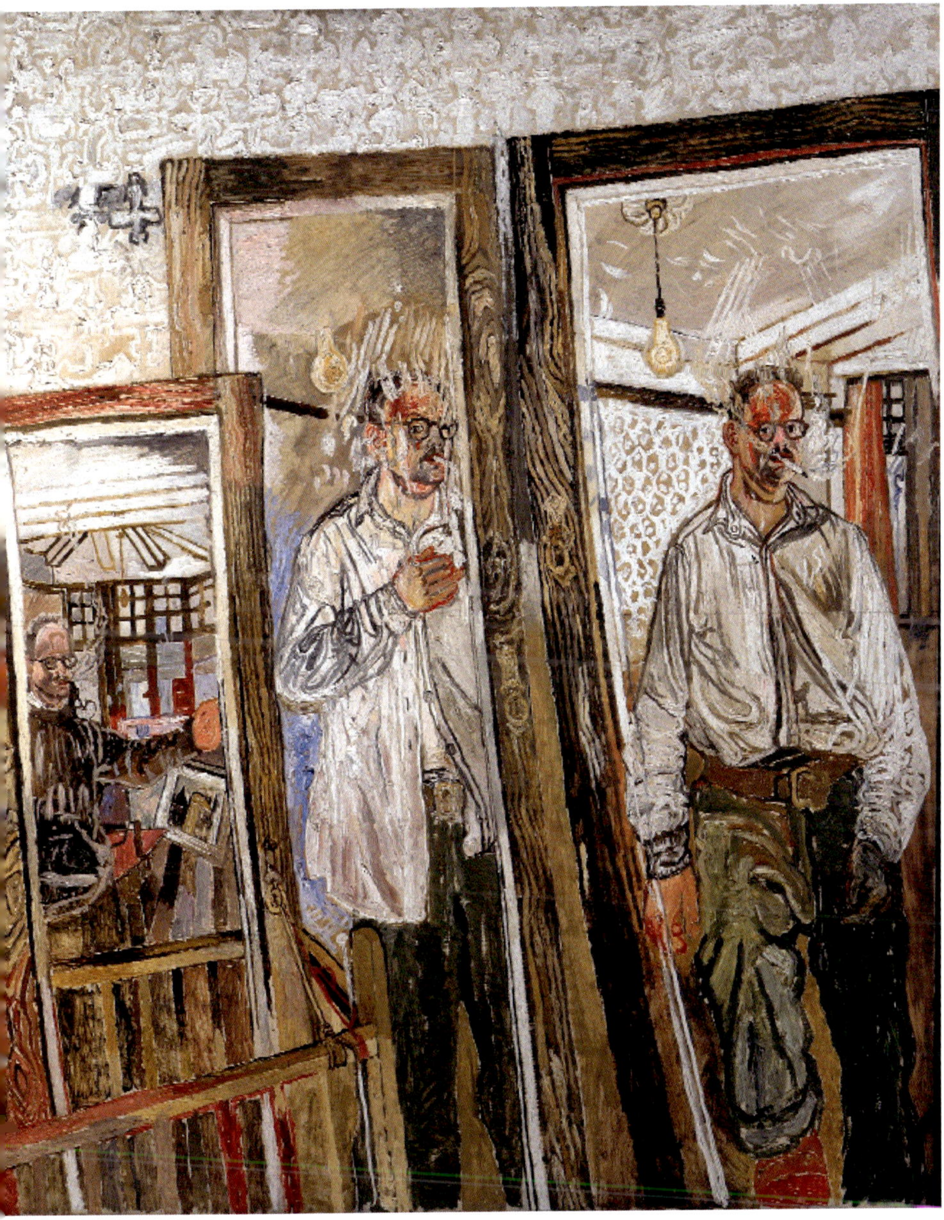

Pin-Up 1963, for Francis Bacon, 1963, Sam Walsh (1934-89)

PIN-UP

Plum like, your eye swells a fleshy
murky purple, that will soon bruise gold.

Lips remain smooth, neat,
the dark crack between them

harbouring exotic smells.
Did someone pincer

a mussel from its shell,
drop it in your mouth

as you waited, a hungry gull?
Did they whisper into thick

sticky roots of your hair
things to make you forget me?

Unsettled by such swagger, did jealous fists
cause your cheeks to marble so?

Sway close to me, let me draw
the night's adventures from your face.

Rebecca Goss

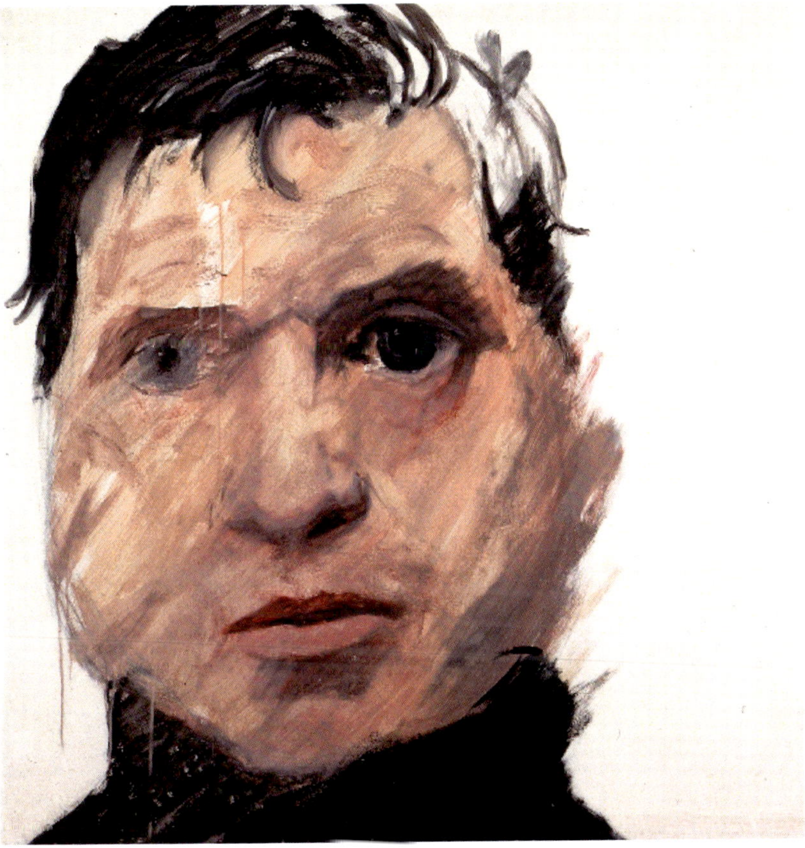

Meat Painting II – In Memoriam Rene Magritte, 1967,
Adrian Henri (1932-2000)

AT THE BUTCHER'S

Body bent, I journey
the glass display,

pause at kidneys,
blood filled stones

gleaming like unctuous
jewels. Shiny cuts,

veined with maps of fat,
invite me to tour each wet

and heavy tray. Eventually,
a chop is lifted, bleeding

watery pink juices
into an experienced palm,

lain gently as a newborn
on waiting scales,

ready to be swaddled
in waxy gingham wrap.

Rebecca Goss

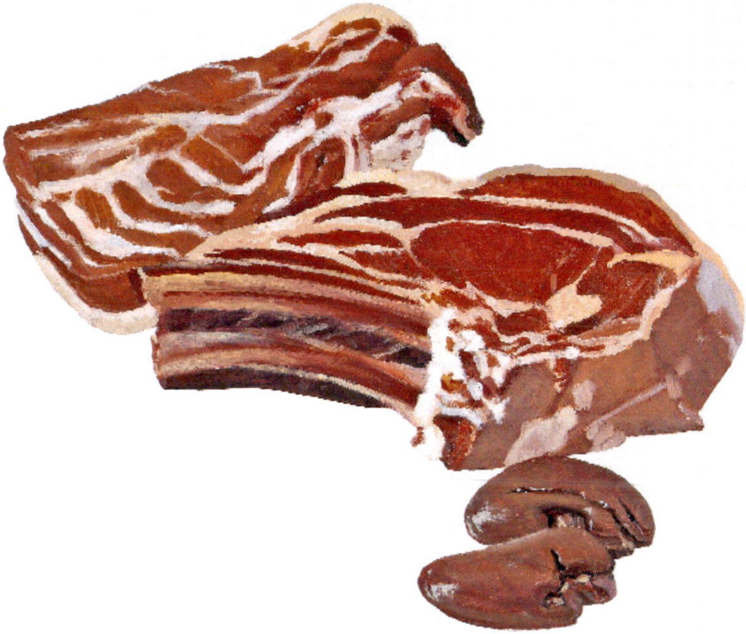

Cow Mutations, 1987, Tim Head

ETCETERA

We graze for hours through the densely structured arguments
about what is and what is not, the genesis of patterns framed
and hung for all to see. But we are prisoners.

Have taken for granted that a fundamental mark
of our distinction is the time somebody takes to understand
that we are not the cut-out clouds they thought, constrained
by all their own subjective contours, not mere inkblots
or the accidental shape of cattle, chiaroscuro cows abstracted
into analogues of what a glance reveals, but prisoners.

Some days we are reduced to inference, can only dream
the great stampede, of thundering through the landscapes
room by room, can only hope that there will be someone
to see us more than mere etceteras.

And in the evening, when everyone has gone,
when the walls we hang upon are being washed and hoofprints
scrubbed out of the polished floors, a portrait of a woman comes
with fists of grass. Now eat, she says. We do. Now, carrying a glass
of painted raindrops, drink. We drink.

Brian Wake

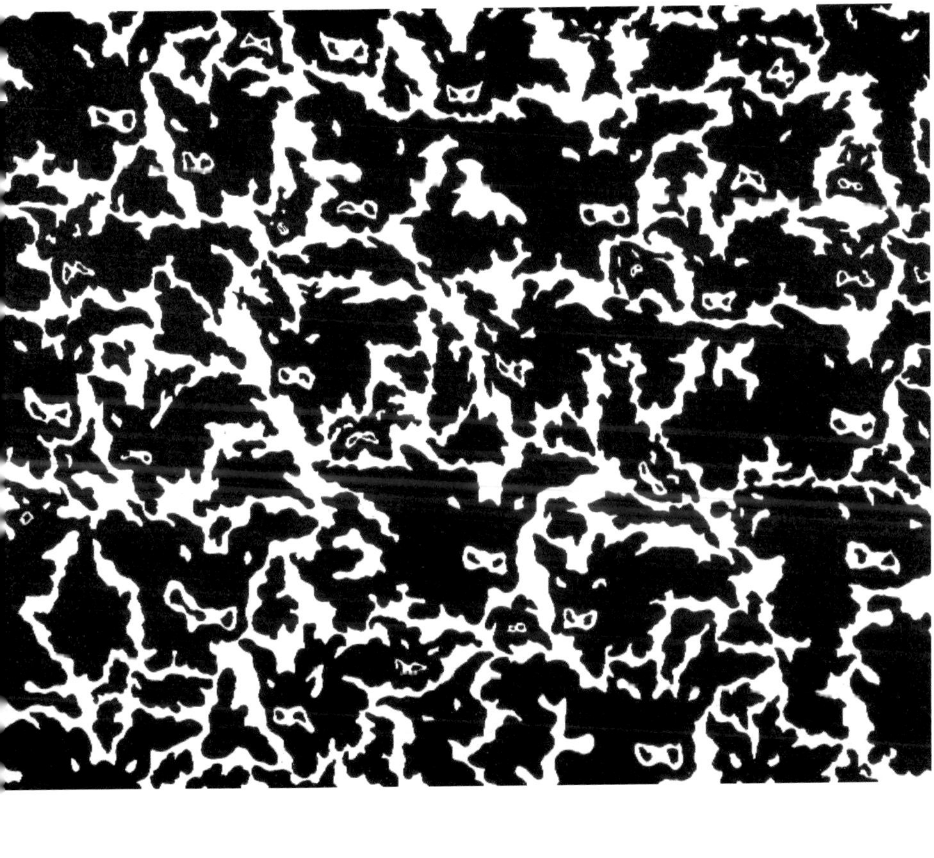

Blotter, 1993, Peter Doig

BLOTTER

Passing by – I see him
standing on ice
    looking down
absorbed in his own reflection.
I want to cry
    There's water on the pond!
    There's water on the pond!
But no words come.
The swirling world below his feet
is now reality, its submerged figure him
and he the ghost.

Relics of colour, violet
green, gold…high banks
of snow, stricken woods
hang cold and lovely.

One last look and he is gone.

But reality, today, is an Art Gallery
where I'm happy to see him
                                        warm the ice.
Where I hope he went back home, whistling.
(Whooping across sheer heaven is 'Brill',
'Cool' and great fun). Where I see
the artist gave him boots, gloves
blue fleece
and flaming headband – to bring
a Canadian winter to life.

I want to murmur,
    Enjoy yourself, lad.
    Go for it!
But only smile.

Gina Riley

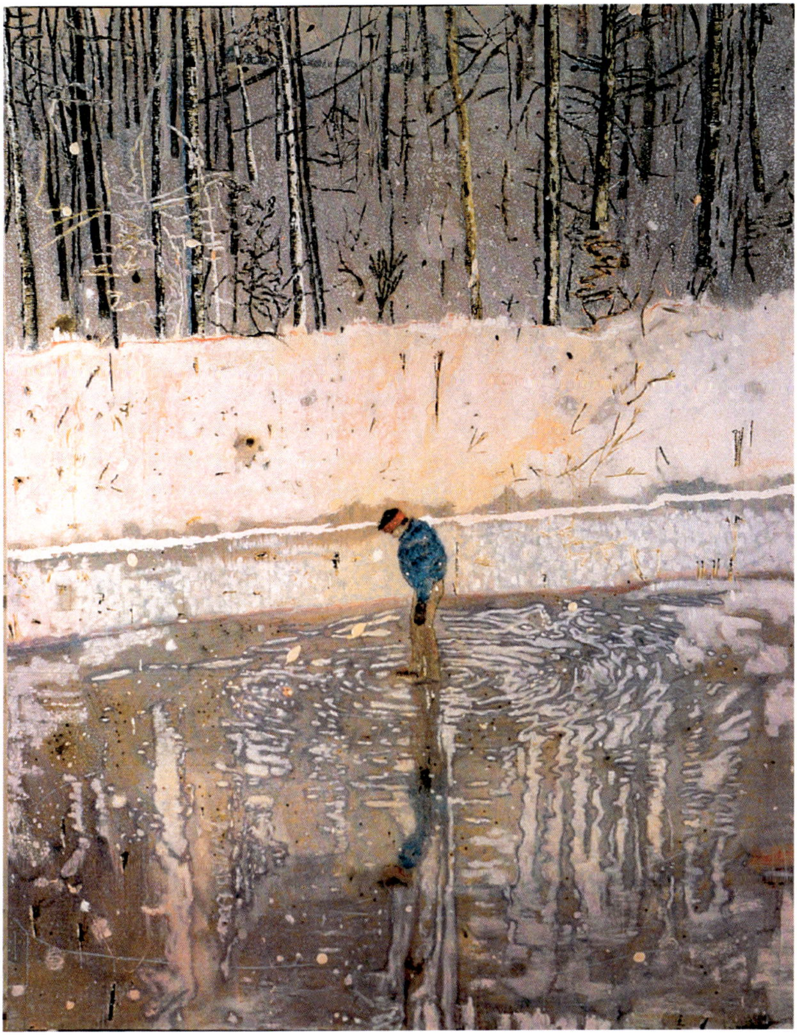

Before Vermeer's Clouds, 2006, Martin Greenland

THE LATTE MUG CAFÉ

I'd doubts about a holiday in paradise. An eternity was definitely out. *Eyes not seen, nor ears heard...*one of the brochures said. *Free virgins...* promised another. Well, I'd learnt from experience that generalities meant listeria in the kebabs and limp lettuce... and, would I not feel guilty about those virgins? Heaven would be an eternity of bad sex for them – poor loves.

My paradise was a snooze in a comfy bed. Unthreatening dreams lulled me. Normally I was snorkelling with the Queen off Torremolinos. I could hear myself snore, and not give a fig. I was asleep, but not dead to the world.

So when Death arrived in the shape of a National Express bus coming the right way up a motorway entrance while I rode my Honda 50 the wrong way, there I was in this beautiful landscape on the banks of a delicious torrent, surveying a lovely city.

'What have we here?' my companion asked. His name was Dawkins.

'Aren't you the chap who...?'

'Shhh!'

'Actually, I'm surprised. I took your books for gospel.'

'What happens now?'

'Isn't it all a bit of a mystery,' I said. 'Like life?'

'No. It's a combination of dying compounds in our brains producing an effect similar to that of lysergic acid diethylamide.'

'Dream on! Have you tasted that torrent?'

Dawkins did so. 'Superb! Similar to the white chocolate mousse at 'The Ivy'.'

We gazed at the city. 'Have you noticed how all four seasons bathe this one view?' Dawkins asked.

'Yes. A bit like Dubai with imagination.'

'I don't believe it!'

We took a stroll. I came upon a golden cupboard. The door slid open and a note inside said: 'Make your way to The Latte Mug Café where you will be assigned the villa of your choice.'

'How do we get there?'

I saw my Honda heading toward me, riderless but pristine.

We hopped on, and the Honda rode us to a high tower that looked exactly like the striped Latte mug I had bought at Whittard of Chelsea – Birkenhead branch. The Honda stopped. The café door opened and a fanfare of coffee aromas sounded.

Dawkins opted for a villa in Summertown, while I went for a modest semi with an immodest balcony in Winterton. This really Pre-Raphaelite angel handed us the keys, wishing us a pleasant eternity.

'What happens now?' Dawkins asked.

'A good question, Dawkins,' the angel said. 'Surprise yourself!'

'And me?'

'Have a Latte. And when you're tired of Lattes, you can dream until hell freezes over. How does that sound?'

'Really lovely,' I said.

I've called my villa 'Happy Endings'. Dawkins, who often comes around, is most comfortable in 'Serene and Befuddled'. Most days we walk together from Winter to Autumn and back – an easy stroll. Thank heavens there is not a sign of those poor virgins. Rumour has it they're in a safe house close to The Latte Mug Café.

Michael Carson

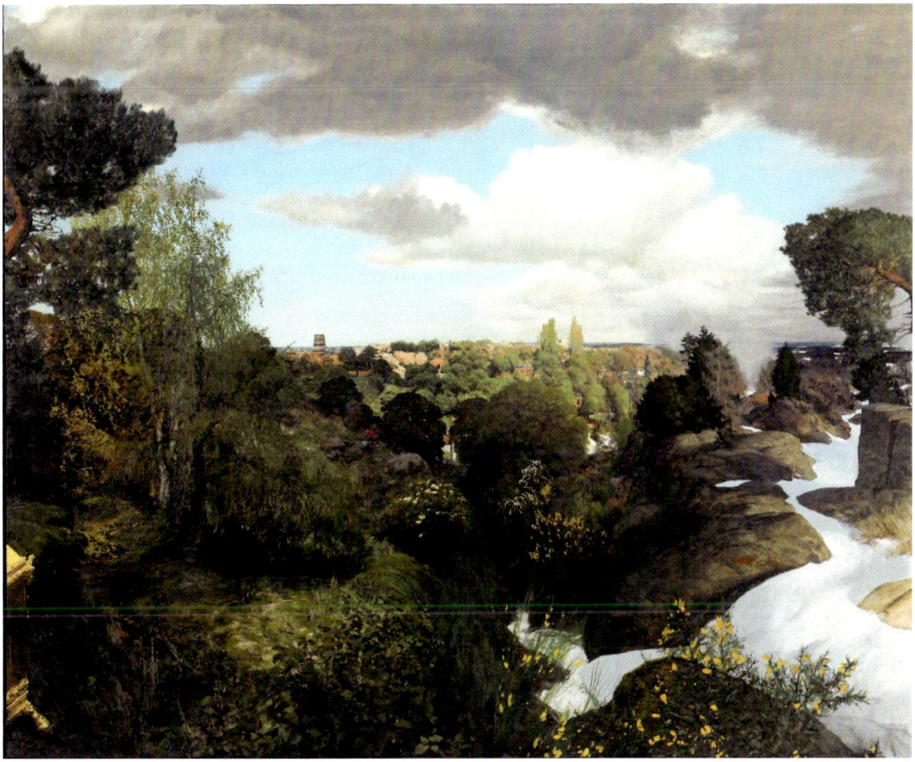

INDEX OF POETS